THE MISSION OF GOD

THE WITNESSING CHURCH SERIES
William J. Danker, Editor

THE
MISSION OF GOD

An Introduction to a Theology of Mission

BY GEORG F. VICEDOM

*Translated by Gilbert A. Thiele
and Dennis Hilgendorf*

CONCORDIA PUBLISHING HOUSE

Saint Louis

Concordia Publishing House, St. Louis, Missouri
Concordia Publishing House Ltd., London, W. C. 1
© 1965 Concordia Publishing House

Library of Congress Catalog Card No. 65-22814

MANUFACTURED IN THE UNITED STATES OF AMERICA

FOREWORD

In the ecumenical discussion of the theology of missions, Prof. Vicedom's book *Missio Dei* has already played an important part. It was hailed at its publication in Germany as the first major study of the subject since the work of Gustav Warneck. As its title indicates, it is a radically theological statement of the source, motive, and end of missions. It takes as its starting point the affirmation of the Willingen Conference that "the missionary movement of which we are a part has its source in the Triune God Himself." It seeks at every point for Biblical foundations. As the author says in his Preface, it tries to help readers "listen to what the Bible has to tell us about the purpose of church work and about the mission."

The book is not intended for the casual or speculative reader. It is, says Professor Vicedom, "intended to offer guidance to missionaries and pastors." It is intended for those who are on the job, and it deals with issues which the working missionary has to face and on which he has to make decisions. He will find here solid material for the making of decisions.

He will not, of course, always agree. The debate has moved on since the book was written eight years ago. But what is here written will repay the thorough and reflective study of those who are wrestling with the new questions which are being put to the church today about missionary principles, methods, and structures.

The translators and the publishers have earned the gratitude of English-speaking Christians for making available to them this important work.

LESSLIE NEWBIGIN

Geneva
February 8, 1965

EDITOR'S NOTE

The original suggestions to translate Georg F. Vicedom's *Missio Dei* came from my mentor and colleague Victor Bartling. Some time later, on a visit to Concordia Seminary, Bishop Lesslie Newbigin strongly urged us to see that this task was carried out for the benefit of the English-speaking world. It was no small labor that was thus initiated. Dennis Hilgendorf, now a missionary in the Middle East at Beirut, Lebanon, did an annotated basic translation in partial fulfillment of the requirements for an advanced degree in Concordia Seminary's Graduate School. Thereupon, Gilbert Thiele, head of Concordia's department of historical theology, kindly reworked the original translation. Further revision was undertaken in line of duty by this appreciative — and perspiring — editor, who has in the process gained new respect for the complex task of rendering scholarly theological German into English that is both faithful and endurable. We are most grateful to the translators for their long hours of toil, to Bishop Newbigin for his gracious Foreword, and to Otto A. Dorn and Roland Seboldt of Concordia Publishing House for their persisten encouragement. Frederick Norden rendered valuable assistance in the preparation of the Index.

We believe that all involved in these labors feel rich satisfaction in having had a part in sharing with a wider circle Georg F. Vicedom's profound and stimulating Biblical thought about the theology of the church on God's mission.

WILLIAM J. DANKER

February, 1965

PREFACE

It is admittedly a bold venture on my part to write an introduction to the present-day theology of missionary work. But since no German theologian has, so far, rendered the mission this service, the need for me to do so is urgent. Except for some essays which are hard to come by, we in Germany have nothing presenting a reasoned justification of the mission which would clearly set forth the changes in missionary thinking. This monograph, then, is intended to offer guidance to missionaries and pastors. On the other hand, the present situation demanded such a study. We shall never achieve any missionary results from our theology and church work unless we allow Holy Scripture to give us the necessary missionary impetus. Only when we have grasped the fact that the whole purpose of the Bible is the rescue of mankind and therefore mission work, only then do theological thought and every type of church work receive their proper direction. This monograph is intended to help toward that end.

Under the pressure of time the task provided both joy and concern. Joy, because over and over again it led me back to sane thinking in my activity in the science of missions. Concern, because it clearly revealed theological gaps. I am aware that in a number of sections the latest theological literature should have been consulted. The urgency of the situation in the current plight of the church in the world, however, precludes postponing publication any longer.

Therefore I present this monograph to the public with the plea not to look for what might have been expected but to listen to what the Bible has to tell us about the purpose of church work and about the mission.

I would like to thank my friend Eduard Haller for his review of the manuscript and for a fruitful exchange of theological thought.

GEORG F. VICEDOM

Neuendettelsau, Bavaria, Seminary

November 17, 1957

On the day of David Zeisberger's death

CONTENTS

INTRODUCTION

We live in an age that devaluates all products of historical development. This is true also in theology. In connection with our theme the question repeatedly arises: Did Jesus intend the church and her mission and are both legitimate dimensions of the Gospel? Although this question has always been addressed to the mission, what is remarkable in this age of ecclesiology is that this question should also be put to the church, the vehicle of the mission. Such an expansion of the question is an unavoidable necessity. The mission is not an independent dimension but can always and only be the result of the church's obedience to the Gospel. Thus, to question the legitimacy of the mission is to question the right of the church itself to exist.

It is impossible within the scope of this study to present a new, authoritative justification of the church. But since the mission cannot be isolated as a separate entity, it follows that the definition of the mission here attempted will also include references to the establishment of the church and its task. It is still an open question whether perhaps it might have been preferable to reverse the procedure. However, I feel myself neither entitled nor qualified to undertake this.

The justification of the mission is nothing new. Since the days of Justinian von Welz it has been repeatedly attempted. It took its classical form in the German evangelical missiology of Gustav Warneck and his followers. Hardly noticed by scientific theology, constantly attacked by the multitude of unbelieving and indifferent people, made the butt of jokes and ridicule by a sensation-seeking press, often endangered by totalitarian governments, the mission has over and over again been forced to prove its Biblical right to exist. For that reason it has until recently taken a defensive position. But today a great change has occurred. Though we may still hear of justifications for the mission today, they no longer attempt to justify the mission with theological argument or even under certain circumstances with secondary arguments, as Warneck did, but they speak of its autonomy and of the commitment to the mission. There is an obvious shift from an anthropocentric to a theocentric approach. This is undoubtedly a result of dialectical theology and its rediscovery of the Reformation message. A new joy in witnessing has come to the church.

Nevertheless, it must be asserted that in Germany, in spite of the detailed rethinking of the mission in Karl Barth's *Church Dogmatics,* theology has remained sterile and impervious with respect to missions. Theology restricted itself in large part to defining and establishing the content of the witness, but did not allow itself to be addressed by God in sufficient measure to achieve a missionary dynamic. Subjectivism has had such wide influence today that no one can say anymore what is the faith of Christendom by which the church lives (Tambaram).[1] Therefore this faith can not be propagated. The church's proclamation and activity are dissipated in nervous spasms. Finally one is forced to ask whether the mission still has a right to exist.

All this has a dire effect on the mission. Since the mission is not an entity in a class by itself, but always only an essential trait and expression of the life of the church, the faults of the church and of theology are symptomatically evident in the mission. Thus every justification for the mission must

[1] This is a reference to the Tambaram Series, *The Authority of the Faith,* a report of the International Missionary Council, Tambaram, India, 1938. Tambaram is a suburb of Madras.

2

touch the basic faults of the church. Only a person who is expert in every branch of theology could undertake this task comprehensively. Hence we must take the other course: To work out a self-understanding of the mission without losing ourselves in endless debates.

Perhaps in this way it is also possible to help the church find her way to a new self-understanding. In Scandinavia, The Netherlands, and Switzerland significant beginnings along these lines have been made. In the following chapters we want to treat chiefly the Dutch findings because they deal most vigorously with the weakness of German theology and with German thinking on the mission. We have been under attack since 1945. The criticism has been very helpful and fruitful, even though it went too far and was given no consideration by German theology.

> We are told that we are guilty of an evaluation of folk and folkways which has its roots in Romanticism, that this has led to an ideology sympathetic to nationalism, that it resulted in many deviations from the basic Biblical position on church and mission, that it eliminated the eschatological factor, and that it finally led to this that the community (congregation) is regarded only as the "extension of the people" and folkways, as a "blessing-bestowing realization of the ethnic structure." [2]

An answer to these serious charges must be found. We are not trying to defend ourselves against the individual charges. Anyone interested in such an approach can consult the cited article by Knak. We prefer to take up these very fruitful suggestions and attempt, in a critical debate with them, to build up a new justification for the mission and for the remaining tasks assigned to the church. As to method we will always develop the pertinent Biblical material first and then proceed to a comparison.

---

[2] Siegfried Knak, "Oekumenischer Dienst in der Missionswissenschaft" [Ecumenical Service in Missiology], *Theologia Viatorum* (1950), p. 157.

THE MISSIO DEI

ARLIER JUSTIFICATIONS of the mission suffered chiefly from the following defects: either they attempted to prove that the mission was justified on the basis of missionary thought in the Bible, and possible and necessary among the nations; or they derived the mission from the church as a secondary assignment or even connected it with the spreading of "Christian" culture.[1] We do not wish to discuss such secondary justifications any further. But not even the apologetic approach does justice to Scripture. The former accentuates the mission as a special work demanded by God. However, the Bible in its totality ascribes only one intention to God: to save mankind.

Therefore the service of the mission cannot be derived from the task of the church. Every task of the church makes sense and has a purpose only as it leads to the mission. The rapprochement of church and mission is a welcome development, and in many parts of the world mission and church are identical. Yet the danger of missionary inactivity and the misunderstanding of the mission are not thereby eliminated.

There is danger that the church itself may become the point of departure, the purpose, the subject of the mission. This is not, however, in accord with Scripture, since it is always the Triune God who acts, who makes His believers

---

[1] Cf. the copious bibliographical notes in Walter Holsten, *Das Kerygma und der Mensch* (Munich: Chr. Kaiser Verlag, 1953), pp. 24 ff. and 32 ff.

members of His kingdom.[2] Even the church is only an instrument in the hands of God. The church herself is only the outcome of the activity of God who sends and saves.

The Conference at Willingen[3] accepted the concept of *missio Dei* to describe this fact.

> The mission is not only obedience to a word of the Lord, it is not only the commitment to the gathering of the congregation; it is participation in the sending of the Son, in the *missio Dei*, with the inclusive aim of establishing the lordship of Christ over the whole redeemed creation.[4] The missionary movement of which we are a part has its source in the Triune God Himself.[5]

1. The Concept

The mission is work that belongs to God. This is the first implication of *missio Dei*. God is the Lord, the One who gives the orders, the Owner, the One who takes care of things. He is the Protagonist in the mission. When we ascribe the mission to God in this way, then it is withdrawn from human whims. Hence we must show that God wants the mission and how He Himself conducts it. This draws all necessary boundaries. The mission, and with it the church, is God's

[2] Wilhelm Andersen, *Auf dem Wege zu einer Theologie der Mission* (Gütersloh: Bertelsmann, 1957), pp. 30 ff. Published first in English as the second in a series of International Missionary Council research pamphlets under the title *Towards a Theology of Mission* (London: SCM Press, n. d.). Andersen is rector and professor of systematic theology at the Augustana Hochschule in Neuendettelsau, Bavaria.

[3] The fifth International Missionary Council conference was held in Willingen, Germany, July 1952. The report of that conference is edited by Norman Goodall in *Missions Under the Cross* (London: Edinburgh House Press, 1953).

[4] K. Hartenstein, "Theologische Besinnung," *Mission zwischen Gestern und Morgen*, ed. W. Freytag (Stuttgart: Evangelischer Missionsverlag, 1952), p. 54.

[5] Goodall, p. 189.

very own work. We cannot speak of "the mission of the church," even less of "our mission." Both the church and the mission have their source in the loving will of God. Therefore we can speak of church and mission always only with the understanding that they are not independent entities. Both are only tools of God, instruments through which God carries out His mission. The church must first in obedience fulfill *His* missionary intention. Only then can she speak of *her* mission, since her mission is then included in the *missio Dei*.

Now our theme is seen in its truly serious dimensions. If it is true that God intends the mission since he Himself carries out the mission, then the church can be God's vessel and tool only if she surrenders herself to His purpose. If she dissociates herself from this concern of God, she becomes disobedient and can no longer be church in the divine sense. "There is no participation in Christ without participation in His mission to the world." [6] Hence the church is not called on to decide whether she will carry on the mission or not. She can only decide for herself whether she wants to be church. She cannot determine when, where, and how missions will be carried out, for the mission is always divinely guided, as is shown us above all in Acts. Mission as the business of God implies that He lays claim to make use of all His believers exactly as He wishes, in order to impart His love to all men through His believers. God makes this claim clear by first achieving the mission *through Himself*. The church can only follow in achieving what God has already done and is doing. She can only point to what He will do. Thus mission is based on the activity of God Himself.

[6] Ibid., p. 190.

6

2. The Mission Through God

If we want to do justice to the Biblical conception, *missio Dei* must be understood also as an attributive genitive. God becomes not only the Sender but simultaneously the One who is sent. Thus Catholic dogmatics since Augustine speaks of sendings or the *missio* within the Triune God.

> On the basis of an intra-divine order of origin one understands the sending as the imparting of one divine Person through Another to the creatures.[7]

Every sending of one Person results in the presence of the Other. Evangelical theology does not treat these sendings as an independent doctrine since it sees danger that God's essential unity might become unthinkable. Rather it tries to grasp the processes immanent in the Trinity by God's relationship to man. However, a number of hymns have kept alive in the evangelical Christian an appreciation of the trinitarian nature of God's sending. For example:

> He spoke to His beloved Son:
> 'Tis time to have compassion.
> Then go, bright Jewel of My crown,
> And bring to man salvation . . .[8]

> "Go forth, My Son," the Father saith,
> "And free men from the fear of death," . . .
> "Yea, Father, yea, most willingly,
> I'll bear what Thou commandest;" . . .[9]

These and other verses describe the above-mentioned sending within the Trinity. They remind us again of the actual motif of the mission.

[7] M. Schmaus, *Katholische Dogmatik* (Westheim: Gangholf Ross Verlag, 1948), I, p. 377. Prof. M. Schmaus, graduate of the University of Munich and author of an eight-volume *Dogmatik,* is a professor at his alma mater.

[8] Cf. *The Lutheran Hymnal* (St. Louis: Concordia Publishing House, 1941), Hymn 387, v. 5.

[9] Ibid., Hymn 142, vv. 2, 3.

We are thus face to face with one of the ultimate mysteries of God, which is perceptible only in God's dealings with men. The highest mystery of the mission out of which it grows and lives is: God sends His Son; Father and Son send the Holy Ghost. Here God makes Himself not only the One sent, but at the same time the Content of the sending, without dissolving through this Trinity of revelation the equality of essence of the divine Persons. For in every Person of the deity God works in His entirety. That process of the intra-divine sending is of eminent significance for the mission and work of the church. The church's commission is prefigured in the divine; her work is there assigned. The meaning and content of her work is determined by the *missio Dei*.

At the same time through His mission God shows Himself to be Lord. He does not allow anyone to dictate to Him. Neither the religious nor the unbelievers can prescribe for Him what He can and cannot do. It is part of the deity of God that He is subject to no human restrictions. He thus imposes tasks on Himself in a manner inaccessible to human concepts. God's activity lies *extra nos*.[10] Thus particularly *missio Dei*, as projected in the doctrine of the Trinity, becomes the expression of the unique government of God. Mohammed, for example, did not understand this when he attempted to restore God in His unity and transcendence by denying the deity of Christ and of the Holy Ghost. He actually degraded God and took from Him the fullness of His revelation and essence.

3. God's Saving Activity and His Sending

Holy Scripture is not interested in speculation. It always reveals God only to the extent that it is important to do so in the interest of His dealing with men. God makes statements in Scripture concerning Himself only as they are nec-

[10] Holsten, p. 44.

essary for the salvation of mankind. Therefore all revelation of God in His *missio* takes place always for the sake of the salvation of mankind. But while He reveals Himself through His activity, He at the same times makes statements concerning man, places him under His judgment, and thereby enables His messengers to bring to mankind both the content of the sending and, thereby, the salvation of mankind. The mission can be nothing else than the continuation of the saving activity of God through the publication of the deeds of salvation. This is its greatest authority and supreme commission.

This saving activity of God, as proffered through the *missio Dei*, His relationship to the world, His dealing with men, is described in Scripture by the word "sending." It is in fact the sum and substance of God's creativity and activity. Thus the entire *Heilsgeschichte* [11] exhibits itself as a history of *missio Dei*.[12] We therefore do no violence to the Scriptures if we start with this term in an attempt to outline the assignment of the church. Furthermore, we remain within the framework of genuine theology, which, of course, can never be a thought-system about God, but which should always and only describe the activity of God in history.[13]

[11] The term has been rendered "redemptive history" or "history of salvation," but it is best taken as a technical term and left in the original language. It stands in contrast to a totally secular view of history and conveys the idea that God is at work in the events of history as He works out His plan of salvation.

[12] Karl Heinrich Rengstorf, ἀπόστολος and ἀποστέλλειν, *Theologisches Wörterbuch zum Neuen Testament*, ed. Gerhard Kittel, I (Stuttgart: W. Kohlhammer Verlag, 1931), pp. 397—448, esp. 402—405. Rengstorf is professor of New Testament Interpretation at the University of Münster, Westphalia, West Germany.

[13] Oscar Cullmann, *Christus und die Zeit* (Zurich: Zollikon, 1946), p. 19. *Christ and Time, the Primitive Conception of Time and History*, tr. Floyd V. Filson (Philadelphia: Westminster Press, 1950). Cullmann is professor of New Testament Interpretation and Early Christian History at the University of Basel, Switzerland, and professor of Early Christianity at the Sorbonne in Paris.

If for the time being we defer discussion of the special *missio Dei* in Jesus Christ and in the gift of the Holy Ghost, as well as of the sending of the prophets and apostles, we still have many passages describing the *missio Dei*. God even sends out entirely impersonal realities and tells us that also by such means he brings his direct influence to bear on the world. For example, He sends a sword to pursue His people (Jer. 9:16), He sends grain and wine, also oil (Joel 2:19), thus revealing Himself in His sending as a God of love. Hence He sends especially to His chosen people goodness and faithfulness (Ps. 57:4), goodness and truth (Ps. 43:3), His Word (Ps. 107:20), a hunger for His Word (Amos 8:11), His redemption (Ps. 111:9). Accordingly through His sending He sustains the world and guides mankind. He exemplifies Himself as a God who has not excluded His creation from His care.

God is always present in this sending. Sending is therefore an expression of His presence at work in judgment and grace. Thus the *missio* becomes a testimony to His deity. God would not be the God of mankind if He were not near the world and active in a way relevant to it. He would be subject to the same fate that befell all man-made creator-gods, who at best exist only in the memory of mankind but are realities no longer.

God, however, has over and over again proved that He releases nothing and no one from His lordship. Through His sending He confronts all mankind in His deity. All people must deal factually with Him who sustains the creation by what He does. His sending becomes a special revelation where it becomes the word to the people (Ps. 19:1-7; 8-11), and in Jesus Christ, in whom He makes a gift to mankind of the Redeemer. Here the same objective fact serves to establish the *missio*, from which Holsten deduces his basis for the science of missiology: "Briefly stated, this basis is the New

Testament kerygma, the proclamation of the decisive activity of God in Christ which in turn calls for decision." [14]

Thus God's *missio* is always at the same time a call into decision. Whether occurring personally or impersonally, His activity is always a messenger that conveys the call. His impact is always an order which demands response. No one can evade this call or inattentively disregard it. God's activity always places man under an obligation (Acts 14:17; Rom. 1:8). Therefore one who declines to put himself at the disposal of *missio Dei* attempts to restrict God in the work designed to serve the world and rescue mankind, in His lordship. The privilege, full authority, commission, and obligation of the mission always flows from the activity of the triune God Himself.

> So long as a cult is being spread only among fellow-countrymen, even though it be away from home, God is Lord only for one tribe or for one city. But if real mission work is carried on the idea of the absolute lordship is attained.[15]

This *missio Dei,* embracing the entire activity of God, can therefore also be equated with the lordship of God.

[14] Holsten, p. 43.

[15] W. Foerster, *Herr ist Jesus* (Gütersloh: C. Bertelsmann Verlag, 1924), p. 78.

[II]

THE LORDSHIP OF GOD

1. The Missionary Motif

THE JUSTIFICATION of the mission by means of the lordship of God is nothing new. Zinzendorf already used it as a starting point. The line of thought carried over through Pietism to Gustav Warneck. For him the rule of God was but *one* thought by which the mission could *also* be justified. His concern was to free the mission from pietistic narrowness, which had interpreted the kingdom-of-God idea as being individualistic and thus wanted to win only those who had been called to the Kingdom. The idea of the kingdom of God was taken up primarily into American theology. And the American missions believed the Kingdom of God was to be realized through social service. That is why German missiological scholarship became very cautious in the use of the term.

It was felt that the use of the kingdom-of-God concept, onesidedly usurped as a basis for the mission, had a restraining influence. This was a mistake. W. Luetgert is the only one who made any attempt to show how the kingdom of God is realized also in world history, giving world history content and goal, and how God's kingdom and activity go hand in hand when he who belongs to the Kingdom also allows himself to become involved in social service.[1] As the Dutch show

---

[1] W. Lütgert, "Reich Gottes und Weltgeschichte," 1928; "Das Reich Gottes und die Mission," *Neue Allgemeine Missionszeitschrift*, 1927, pp. 97 ff.

us today, we would have achieved the needed eschatological viewpoint if we had earnestly busied ourselves with the kingdom-of-God concept.[2] Stimulated by this insight, in a day when all missionary motifs have proved themselves inadequate, the German missionary enterprise is again returning to this kingdom basis.[3] The missionary motif is always concerned with the question: Why must we do missionary work? Formerly the simplest answer was: God wants to save all men. To be sure, even today this answer still retains its validity. However, today other religions also are offering man salvation and solution for the problems of his life. They are contesting the claim of the Christian proclamation. At the very least, this raises further questions such as these: Why does God want to save mankind? Has He a right to this claim? What sort of a reply do we owe the other religions? What is the goal of redemption and of the mission?

Hence one can no longer substantiate the mission in the way which Holsten uses when he justifies missiology.[4] He proceeds solely from the motif. This, however, becomes adequate only when the goal is constantly kept in mind at the same time.[5] Today we are trying to find the answer by seeking the basis for the mission in the royal lordship of God. Let us see whether an answer so attained can be harmonized with basic thinking about the *missio Dei.*

[2] A discussion of missionary motivation can be found in W. Freytag, "Vom Sinn der Weltmission," *Evangelische Missionszeitschrift,* 1950, pp. 1 ff.

[3] Cf. Siegfried Knak, "Oekumenischer Dienst in der Missionswissenschaft," *Theologia Viatorum,* 1950, pp. 157 f.

[4] Cf. ch. II, footnote 14.

[5] Wilhelm Andersen, "Die kerygmatische Begründung der Religions- und Missionswissenschaft," *Evangelische Missionszeitschrift,* 1954, pp. 29 ff. Hendrik Kraemer, *Religion and the Christian Faith* (London: Harper, 1956), pp. 196 ff.

13

It is my opinion that one can grasp God's activity with mankind as objectively under the heading "kingdom of God" as under *"missio Dei."* Both concepts to be sure do not describe the same procedure, but they have a great deal in common. If we see the *missio Dei* substantiated in the truth that God is God, then surely the lordship of God has the same ultimate basis. The goal of the *missio Dei* is to incorporate mankind in the βασιλεία τοῦ θεοῦ [the kingdom of God], and to convey to mankind the gifts thereof. Justification, which is for Holsten the starting point of all missionary thinking, is not thereby depreciated but included in the totality of God's dealing with mankind.[6] This dealing involves more than declaring man righteous and accepting him into divine fellowship. For with the Kingdom God also gives everything that He does for the justified sinner.

> Justification consists, after all, in nothing less than reception into the kingdom of God. The doctrine of justification should answer only the question: How do we enter the kingdom of God? . . . He who is justified is thereby taken into the service of God.[7]

Thus the kingdom of God might be described as the goal of the *missio Dei.* Another connection is found in the *vis-a-vis* of God [8] which the *missio Dei* as well as the βασιλεία share, i. e. the world of mankind. The working of God in His love toward this *vis-a-vis* is performed with this in mind. Hence we now want to describe this *vis-a-vis* so that the goal of the sending and the gifts of the βασιλεία will become clear.

[6] Walter Holsten, *Das Kerygma und der Mensch* (Munich: Chr. Kaiser Verlag, 1953), pp. 52 ff., 61.

[7] W. Lütgert, "Das Reich Gottes und die Mission," loc. cit.

[8] The term "das Gegenüber Gottes" also translatable as "The opposite number of God" is here generally reproduced as "the *vis-a-vis* of God," in order to avoid the implication of equality of man with God, even before and certainly after the Fall. (Tr.)

2. *God's* Vis-a-Vis

Christianity, in contrast to other religions, emphasizes the fact that God created the world and mankind. This is God's *vis-a-vis*. The world is not an effusion of the Deity and thus a part of Him. Nor did it come into existence through birth. Above all, the world did not originate alongside of Him or against Him, so that it would thus be a force antagonistic to Him. There is no dualism or emanationism involved. These types of explanation, familiar to us in other religions, are completely out of the picture. With mankind, the world is the creation of God brought into existence by His almighty Word in accordance with His will. In other words, God has created a *vis-a-vis*, a "Thou," and thus a place for activity on His part. This was already the case before the Fall. The *imago Dei* [9] can certainly only mean that God created a being *which could have fellowship with Him and therein found life satisfying.*

There was no necessity in this fellowship for a special sending or for emphasis on the lordship of God. The lordship was self-evident. The fellowship God granted to mankind was the βασιλεία of God. Herein man stood under the lordship of God. The *vis-a-vis* of God in this fellowship is once more restored through redemption. This does not imply, however, that in this restoration man would enter the deity as is thought in other religions. Redemption is not return into the deity, but into the proper attitude toward God.

Man fell out of this role of God's *vis-a-vis* in which he

[9] The term implies four definite facets when applied to man by God: (1) communication with God; (2) a status above animal life; (3) power to exercise God's dominion; (4) submission. The last factor must always be there. Man was to realize that he was the *imago* and not the Lord Himself. Failure here is precisely the fall of Adam. The result was that now man begat man in *his* own image. Gen. 5:1, 3 contains the resounding refrain "and he died . . . and he died . . . and he died." Cf. *TWNT*, II, 378—396. (Tr.)

15

was established through creation. Only because man was a creature of God was the Fall possible. Had he been an emanation of God he could not have committed an offense against God or lost his divine character. In other religions therefore we indeed find misdemeanors but no sins, through which man becomes guilty before God. In those other religions sin is always understood as a mistake in behavior over against the divine, by which man harms himself. Sin as offense against God is recognized only where men by revelation know God as Creator and Lord; and there they also need a redeemer.

The relationship between God and mankind was disturbed by the Fall. Man made the *vis-a-vis* role a hostile one. Thus man abandoned the fellowship with God. Man ran away from God and on a level with Him — so he assumes — developed into an independent entity, presumably with the privilege of choosing whether to acknowledge God or not. To assert himself alongside of and against God has become the heart of all his endeavors. He goes to such lengths that he believes he would be doing God a favor if he would return to God. Thus God would become dependent on the grace of man. Sinful man places a question mark behind the lordship of God. But through his nature, determined by the Fall, man now goes on to drag the rest of creation into enmity against God.

However, since sinful man has his real ground of being in his dependence on God, without whom he cannot exist, he seeks to find a substitute by searching for a relationship to the Deity which suits him in a religion of his own making. Even when the religions express thoughts ever so profound, they are giving clear evidence of this development. Again and again they make it apparent that even after the Fall man cannot deny that his destiny lies in fellowship with God. Thus within creation an area has arisen which constantly wants to withdraw itself from the lordship of God and fights against it. The goal and content of the *missio Dei* and the lordship of God is to conquer this hostile area, to bring man once more into the proper place of the *vis-a-vis,* to restore him to fellowship with God, and to liberate him from sin.

At the same time also after the Fall God regards His *vis-a-vis* as His creation. He has for that reason not simply annihilated sinful man, something his rebellious lust for power would have deserved. Rather He remains true to Himself in His relationship to His creatures since the Fall. In long-suffering and patience, through judgment and grace, He is trying to win men back and to bestow on them participation in the βασιλεία. Because of this attitude of God, if for no other reason, we should beware of describing the lordship of God as analogous to the human lust for power.

3. The Other Kingdom

This description does not plumb the gulf caused by the Fall between God and mankind in its enormity and depth. Therefore until now we could not expand upon the grandeur of God's saving activity. Evangelical theology is rather hesitant about placing the realm of the lordship of God alongside of the other realm which is hostile to it. Still we must be aware that we can not speak of the βασιλεία of God without discussing its corresponding opposite, i. e., the dominance to which man has become subject. To all intents and purposes the differentiation between both areas of dominion is the theme of the Sacred Scriptures. We dare not account for this by pointing to the limitations of the Biblical authors and to the fact that they were children of their time. The other realm, too, is a fact and is presented to us in exactly the same way as God in His creation. And so the Bible has in any case the most forceful view of history and the deepest possible understanding of history.

It is not our purpose here to develop a satanology or to

17

explain the origin of evil. We are merely speaking of a fact. Assuredly we are here faced with a mystery. The Bible speaks of a devil without offering explanations as to his ancestry. It speaks of him as of a reality; he is the foe of God and mankind. The realm of the devil has to be overcome (Matt. 4:3; cf. Luke 4:5). It is subject to the prince of this world (John 12:31; 14:30; 16:11). Because his realm unites all antigodly powers in itself, it is a consistent whole (Matt. 12:26; cf. Luke 11:18). The prince of darkness misleads men, moves them to disobedience, and tries to withdraw them from God's control (Eph. 6:11; 1 Peter 5:8). He is the foe of the kingdom of God and thus of its mission, against which he is constantly working (Matt. 13:39; Luke 8:12). While God through His Spirit gives mankind power for a new life which pleases Him, the devil transmits to those who are his the power of evil (John 8:44; Rev. 13:2 ff.). Therefore in the last analysis it is he who misleads mankind to sin and continually turns men into rebels. Actually he exercises dominion in a manner understandable to mankind against the background of sin. With his realm he is God's adversary. That is why Jesus understood the lordship of God and the purpose of His sending to be this that the works of the devil must be destroyed and the prince of this world must be judged (1 John 3:8; John 16:11).

To this we must cling even at the risk of being ridiculed as fundamentalistic. One who does not take these facts into consideration is unfit to carry out the assignment of God. Nor can he understand the ultimate crippling of man and take sin seriously in its actual strength. Never will he be released from the dream that the kingdom of God might be realized on earth, a kingdom which could be constructed by human means. In the last analysis the religions are also to be understood from the viewpoint of their connection with this other kingdom. While they may contain much good, it is imbedded in evil and covered over by evil. Satanic powers hostile to God are at work in them. Only the person who realizes this can experience the properly compassionate judgment about pagan man who is imprisoned in these religions.

The kingdom of the world or the kingdom of the devils as the *vis-a-vis* to the kingdom of God and the *missio Dei* is all the more dangerous since it never puts in an appearance wearing its true face. It seeks to camouflage itself at all times under the mask of good, of that which is proper for man, with goals that are often ideal. That is why the boundary between it and the kingdom of God can only in rare cases be drawn clearly and visibly. In the kingdom of the devils the good intentions of men work themselves out for evil and for destruction. Karl Heim in his discussion of Hendrik Kraemer's book, *The Christian Message in a non-Christian World,* therefore says: "Nothing that God has created is protected from this demonization. Everything can be seized by it. Therefore there is a demonic self-adulation of the ego, the image of God, a demonic sexuality of which man is no longer the master, the demonism of technology, the demonism of power, the demonic degeneration of nationalism. There is a demonism of piety, and prayer itself can get lost in demonic convulsion. As we have experienced in the Pentecostal movement, even the gift of the Holy Ghost can be demonized. The satanic element in the matter lies in this: the demonic power depends entirely on God and what He has created. It possesses nothing that does not come from God. Whatever is demonized and turned against God is always but a distorted image of the glory of God." [10]

In his recent book about religions, Kraemer again and again has penetrated to this final depth of the understanding of world religions. He refers to the fact that neither man in his profound misery nor the religions can be understood with-

[10] K. Heim, "Die Struktur des Heidentums," *Evangelische Missions-Magazin,* 1939, p. 17.

out the power of the evil one, the devil, who turns everything base into light and perverts everything good. "The world of religion and religions (of culture as a whole) belongs to the realm of the 'old man,' the unredeemed man, not yet re-created into the image of God, in whose likeness man was originally created, and therefore, with all its marvelous achievements and satanic deviations, under divine judgment, dimly or unwittingly awaiting its redemption." [11]

However, it is not our assignment to unfold the Biblical understanding of the religions; that would be a task by itself. Here it will be enough to describe that other kingdom which most strongly brings to expression the reality of the lost condition of man. Only he is snatched from the kingdom of this world who permits himself to be rescued from it for the kingdom of God through the sending of Jesus Christ. This is the only way. He is not helped into the Kingdom by the same parentage (Cain and Abel), nor by belonging to the nation (Romans 2), nor by the same employment (Matt. 24:20), nor by the most intimate association of people among them-selves (Luke 17:34), and, we may add, not by membership in the same church. The boundary is drawn only by faith, by membership in the kingdom of God. Men must be called to it by the *missio Dei.*

4. The Kingdom of God

"The kingdom of the world" or "of the devil" is the most comprehensive expression for the lost condition of men, who by their own power can no longer extricate themselves from it nor return into the fellowship of God. Therefore it is the decision of God to help men, to pluck them from the king-dom of darkness, and to transfer them through His *missio* into His kingdom. Thus the kingdom of God becomes not only the opposite number to the kingdom of the devils but

[11] Kraemer, p. 257. See also pp. 321, 337, 378 ff.

at the same time a rallying point for those who have been liberated from their power. Unfortunately Pietism has so narrowed down the concept of the kingdom of God that the kingdom of God and the reign of God consisted only of the sum total of the converted.[12] However, for Warneck the kingdom of God is the antiworldly phenomenon that according to the will of God should embrace all men, which of course is not to say that all men allow themselves to be called into the Kingdom.[13]

Even with this last definition not everything is said, for not only the world of men is subject to the reign of God. This reign does not restrict itself to those who return to the fellowship of God. As a matter of principle God has not freed anything in His creation from the scope of His reign. There is no world which could exist alongside of Him. In the last instance, even the kingdom of the devil must serve His ends. God is King (Ps. 93:1; 99:1) and rules in all the world and over the entire world (Ps. 103:19). God possesses the necessary power, the glory of the royal dignity, the eternal steadfastness. (Matt. 6:13)

However, in the nature of the case as well as in the form of its expression His reign is set in opposition to the kingdom of the world. Therefore, in contrast to the kingdoms of the world, it can be simply described as the kingdom of the heavens. This reign thus functions in a manner opposite to the way things are done on earth. This will become particularly clear when we come to speak about the content of this reign and of its gifts. He rules in righteousness and right proceeds from Him (Ps. 45:7; 49:4). In His kingdom the divisions among men have ceased, there are no racial distinctions, social antagonisms are overcome (Matt. 8:11; Luke

12 W. Freytag, op. cit., p. 2.

13 Gustav Warneck, *Evangelische Missionslehre* (Gotha: F. A. Perthes, 1897), Vol. III, 1, p. 170.

13:29). Therefore this kingdom contains everything which the fellowship with God offers and for which men have longed since the Fall. God fashions this Kingdom for His dealings with men, and together with it gives them their redemption. Therefore the proclamation of the Kingdom through the *missio* is the tidings of great joy. That message is at the same time a call to men and a claim upon them. By this proclamation they are called to God and so to decision, to conversion (Matt. 6:33; Rom. 14:7). God's goal in dealing with men is the Kingdom.

5. *Jesus, the Content of the Kingdom*

This kingdom of God cannot be subsumed in earthly forms, but as long as the kingdom of the world lasts, it possesses an eschatological character. Since the church of God must always live in the world, it can belong to the kingdom of God only to the extent that, unlike the world, it allows itself through faith to be molded by God's kingdom in all aspects of its life. It constantly lives amid longing and hope that this kingdom of God may become reality. God's first answer to this longing was to give His church the Messianic promises and to teach her to wait and hope for the Redeemer. The Kingdom became reality in the appearance of the Messiah, but of course because of its opposition to the kingdom of the world it was different from what men thought it would be. The offence of men and the temptation of God's church remains, for on earth the Messiah did not raise up an earthly kingdom with the marks of the kingdom of God; He revealed to men only the manner of His kingdom. Unless we keep this in mind we will stray on many a wrong path in church and mission.

The kingdom of God cannot become concrete in earthly forms. God, however, makes it concrete for men in this way that he permits His Son to become man, sends the Messiah, and makes Him the bearer of the Kingdom because the Messiah stands and lives in communion with God and thus also with the βασιλεία. He is the one sent in the name of the Lord (Matt. 21:9) to whom all regal honors are due because of his exaltation in the highest heavens (Luke 18:38). He is the King who royally cares for His own and returns to them hundredfold what they have sacrificed for Him (Luke 18:29). There is no power which will not be subject to Him and which He will not destroy when He brings the Kingdom (Matt. 28:19). God's reign and Jesus Christ are one and the same thing. Therefore he who proclaims the name of Jesus also proclaims the reign of God (Acts 8:12; 28:31). Jesus is God's answer to man's quest and therefore the content of the proclamation of the Kingdom (2 Tim. 4:1). All of this is summarized in Colossians [14] where everything that is ascribed to God in the Old Testament is said of Jesus Christ Himself.[15] Of course it has to be pointed out here that the kingdom of God embraces more than the saving acts of Jesus, namely the complete dealing of the Triune God with the world. The Kingdom is above all the activity of God the Father and consequently it is filled with that which we designate as Godhead. Colossians makes this clear.

6. The Otherness of the Kingdom of God

In Jesus Christ it becomes particularly clear that the reign of God is completely different from its opposite, the kingdom of the world. He does not bring men a kingdom of external happiness. He does not even fulfill their wishes which they

[14] No doubt the author has Col. 1:15-20 in mind. Jesus Christ is the image of the invisible God (note the paradox!), the πρωτότοκος, the source of all creation from the highest to the lowest level, the factor that holds all together and keeps it together (the meaning of συνίστημι). He is the κεφαλή, the ἀρχή, the fullness of God. Thus He is at the right hand of God, Col. 3:1. (Tr.)

[15] On the entire matter cf. *TWNT* on βασιλεία, vol. I, pp. 579—592.

believe they have a right to express simply as men. He does not even let them keep the illusion that they will be well off with Him but plainly tells them that they will have to suffer for His sake. He helps no one to attain his worldly goals, but where everything is enfolded by the will of the Father there He is the Helper. Nor does He lead His church out of its alien status in this world, grant her her own state, and unite her on a national basis. He does not reign as an earthly king. His kingdom is divine and therefore withdrawn from the human and demonic sphere of influence which would shape it, but nevertheless it is at work in the world.

It is in opposition to human tendencies (Matt. 11:29). Jesus demonstrates that He is King by bringing men redemption through His death. "The Cross, the actual redemption which has taken place, is not only the solution to the problem of guilt but also to the problem of power, and it is this not just then and there, but already here and now." [16] His kingdom has to be understood soteriologically and therefore has rules entirely different from those of the kingdoms of the world. Therefore no one can enter this kingdom unless he leaves behind all earthly dynastic ideas. Thus participation in the kingdom of Jesus is always tied up with μετάνοια, conversion. He who fails to consider this will always set false goals for himself in church and mission and even while performing the most pious labor will land in the kingdom of the world.

At the same time the kingdom of God is beyond the reach of every human attack and stands outside of all naturalistic ethics and legalism. It also stands outside of every human ideal. On the one hand it is ushered in by God alone by means of the proclamation of the Word and the dispensation of the

[16] K. Hartenstein, "Theologische Besinnung," *Mission zwischen Gestern und Morgen*, ed. W. Freytag (Stuttgart: Evangelischer Missionsverlag, 1952), p. 60.

sacraments, a method of propagation proper to the Kingdom. God binds His *missio* in the sending and transmission through the church to Word and Sacrament. All human devices by which we love to lure men and make the Kingdom palatable to them fall away; for also these are subject to μετάνοια, to reversal, conversion.

On the other hand the Kingdom is also beyond all human legalism in which man believes he can be something before God and can gain something for himself. In the kingdom of God the rankings according to importance emphasized in the kingdom of this world and also widely in the church are in no way normative. He who does not humble himself like a child entirely obedient to his father, will not enter this kingdom (Matt. 18:4). In God's kingdom only he will always have a position who receives his authority from this kingdom. Thus the kingdom of God is also removed from every human attempt to mold it, so that His rule, in contrast to the rule of the world, develops in secret. What would be a defeat for worldly rule is for the reign of God omnipotence and victory. It is fulfilled behind a mask, as Luther said.

Last but not least, the kingdom of God is different because of its eschatological character. A distant goal is bound up with it which enlivens the presence of the Kingdom in Jesus Christ with the great hope of the realization of the Kingdom through the return of Christ. One cannot speak of this kingdom without emphasizing this realization. The Kingdom is a future one in a double sense: (a) At His return Christ will erect the kingdom of God in such a way that God will be all in all, i. e., He will not only conquer the kingdom of this world and of the devil with all its playful attempts at powers but destroy it, so that for all time the conflict in God's creation which was brought about by sin will be eliminated. In Him there will be a new creation. (b) Until the time of His return Christ will have His kingdom proclaimed (Matt. 24:14), gather the members of the Kingdom through the *missio,* place men before the decision, and be present in His church with the gifts of the Spirit until He comes. Thus with His kingdom and with His *missio* Christ has a very distinct goal in history. And it is through the mission that He leads history to its goal. In this way the mission becomes a decisive power, shaping history in the reign of God.

7. The Kingdom of God as Gift

The otherness of the kingdom of God characterizes also the ways of God with men. In its relationship to men the Kingdom does not appear as dominance, coercion, or usurpation, but as a gift which only the Lord of the Kingdom transmits. Moreover, this withdraws it from man's caprice. This gift always remains the giver's to dispose of as he will. Man cannot of himself take possession of it. In this way God again and again removes His kingdom from sin's lust for power. "The kingdom of God shall be taken from you and given to a nation bringing forth the fruits thereof" (Matt. 21:43). God elects but He deposes if His gifts are abused. He bestows but He demands the return of the gift when it is used against Him, so that He can give it to those who will use it in the best interests of the Kingdom.

In His love He always gives His kingdom to those who let themselves be led into it (Luke 12:32). He calls them to His kingship and His glory (1 Thess. 2:12). Basically the Kingdom is a gift. As the Father has given it, so also the Son gives it (Luke 22:29) in order to liberate men from the kingdom of darkness and transfer them into His kingdom (Col. 1:13). Thus service in this kingdom also becomes a gift, a privilege, which is under the rightful control of the bestower.

It is in harmony with the gift and the bestowal that it cannot be forced on anyone. Here, too, the contraposition

26

of God and man is guaranteed. Man has complete freedom of decision to accept the gift or to refuse it. But he cannot steal this kingdom, make it his own, and dispose of it, as many crypto-Christians in pagan lands attempt to do and as nationalists in the younger nations believe, when they hold that they can raise a national claim on Jesus because He belongs to all humanity. Only in accord with the rules of the Kingdom can it be received. One can only let himself be called into it, and only in response to this call, which is always a call to obedience, can one enter it.

The Kingdom thus presupposes a receptive, petitioning, expectant attitude in men (Matt. 10:15; Luke 18:17; Mark 15:43). Only he who has this attitude will receive and inherit the unshakeable kingdom (Heb. 12:28; Matt. 25:34). Thus the reception is also bound up with μετάνοια, conversion. Man must allow God to work at and upon him, he must let himself be renewed by the Spirit of God; then he can become a citizen of the Kingdom. (John 3:5)

These features of the reign of God ought really to be self-evident to every preacher of the Kingdom. Still they are often overlooked. That is why it is so difficult in church and mission today to arrive at a right understanding of sending and service. To a large extent the opposition to the Kingdom of the world has been lost. Often the path to man is sought in assimilation, while only a confrontation would be of help to him.

8. The Kingdom as Rescue

Because the kingdom of God is against the kingdom of the world, God rescues men by His kingdom and at the same time judges the other kingdom and all who belong to it. This is the judgment upon men who live according to the laws of the kingdom of darkness although they knew something of the way to live in the kingdom of God (Rom. 1:18 ff.). This judgment is in effect with the very coming of Jesus. It is intrinsic to the fact that men now have the possibility of rescue. Thus their own unbelief renders judgment upon them (John 3:17 ff.). Still it has a futuristic character with significance for eternity; for Jesus is at the same time the One to whom God transfers judgment at His return. He will prove Himself to be Messiah and King by being the judge of men (Acts 17:32). He pronounces the verdict which men on the basis of their attitude toward the Gospel have spoken against themselves, and He carries it out (John 5:22-29). Through this judgment the proclamation (message) of the Kingdom becomes existential. For those who allow themselves to be called into the Kingdom it becomes a proclamation of rescue, and for those who refuse it a proclamation of damnation.

Through this judgment the Kingdom as a present reality enters into the sharpest possible opposition to the kingdom of the world. There is no accommodation here, only division which must be carried out on the basis of the proclamation of the Kingdom among men. What is suggested in the present kingdom of God (Luke 17:20 ff.) by the line of separation of faith and unbelief is revealed in this that Jesus is the content of the Kingdom as well as the judge because here and now through Him the kingdom of God is judgment upon the other kingdom. This will become apparent in complete clarity in the future kingdom.

If we wish to retain the significance of the kingdom of God and the *missio Dei* as the rescue by God, we must get this eschatological viewpoint with its disturbing sharpness. In judgment God reveals His kingdom of glory and salvation not to initiate paradisiacal conditions on earth but to destroy the world of sin and to produce by means of a new creation full partnership with those who are His own, who have let themselves be rescued through Jesus Christ by the proclamation of the Kingdom. He does it not because of a lust for power, but it proceeds from the innermost attitude of His being, out of love (John 3:16), by which His relationship to the world is described. He does not wish to have men remain in the kingdom of darkness and be lost in it (Col. 1:13). Therefore He sends His Son, who seeks and saves that which is lost. (Matt. 18:11; Luke 19:10)

The Son is the bearer of the Kingdom and gives it its content. He brings men nothing less than the redemption which He has accomplished; He gives them new life through justification and rebirth; He brings His own the eternal life which He has earned for them through death and created through the resurrection. These accomplished redemptive acts are the fulfillment of all salvation preaching on which the coming kingdom bases itself. Since God has reconciled the world with Himself through Christ, He has produced the community which is enfolded by the kingdom of God. Thus all promises have been fulfilled in Jesus Christ. In Him the kingdom of God has come near to men (Matt. 3:2; 4:17; 10:7; Mark 1:15) and has in Him become so present (Luke 17:20), that in the news of salvation God has already let that be proclaimed which has occurred through the Cross and Resurrection.

"Although the Son is the servant of God and because He is that, God makes Him to be the Messiah, i. e., the bearer of the proclamation of the Kingdom and of the will of His kingdom. Now if the Kingdom is everlasting life, then the bearer of the Kingdom must also know about this life. The YES to the reign of God is the YES to the life from God, and therefore the Messiah is He who goes toward the Resurrection. The Messiah is the kingdom of God become present reality, though in veiled and incipient form." [17] We must add that therewith the last word about the reign of God is not yet

[17] Walter Künneth, *Theologie der Auferstehung* (Munich: Claudius, 1951), p. 109. Künneth is professor of Dogmatics at Erlangen University.

spoken. He has turned the Kingdom over to His Son, the Son has actualized it through His suffering and death and in the resurrection He has given men the hope of everlasting life. In this way he has created the preparations for taking over the Kingdom through His ascension. "The end and eschatological turning point is not this resurrection but the exaltation which bestows upon the resurrected one all power in heaven and earth." [18] Now He is the Lord who from His place at the right hand of God calls all men to His kingdom and liberates them from the other kingdom.

9. Present and Future of the Kingdom

The Kingdom has fulfilled itself through the completion of God's saving acts and through the exaltation of Jesus. Only if we recognize this will our proclamation of the *missio Dei* be Biblical. It will always stand in expectation of the return of Christ and point to the coming kingdom, but it can do this only by speaking of Him who has already come in order to give men salvation at the time of His return. If we would speak otherwise we would be removing the Kingdom from history in which it was revealed. But if we were to speak only of the Kingdom to come, we would rob history of its goal and make the preaching of the Kingdom ineffective because it would have no fulfillment. As important as it is to emphasize the latter, we must nevertheless consider that this hope is firmly grounded only if we know that the returning Lord will be no one else than He who has come and has done everything needful for our redemption. Only from the background of this perfect tense can the believer bear witness to the future tense of the judgment and the consummation of the Kingdom. Because of these facts about the Kingdom, and because of its goal, the message of the Kingdom is

[18] E. Lohmeyer, "Mir ist gegeben alle Gewalt," *In memoriam Ernst Lohmeyer*, ed. W. Schmauch (Stuttgart: Evangelisches Verlagswerk, 1951), p. 28.

not devoid of all elements of time and history, as are the mythical pagan religions. Therefore also it cannot be actualized through a dramatic presentation of what has happened, as the pagan myths easily can, but it is a once-for-all thing in its past *and* its future. The revelation of the Kingdom bases itself on historical facts. This is its uniqueness and on these facts it founds its claim to truthfulness. But truth gives the right and the authority for the achievement of the sending.

Things are different for the unbeliever to whom the news of the kingdom of God must first be proclaimed. For him the kingdom of God is not yet here. Chronologically he antedates the Kingdom. It comes to him through the messenger of Jesus, through the proclamation of the news of the Kingdom and thus it approaches him. This is no contradiction; for the kingdom of God can approach a man only because in Jesus Christ it has become a fact. Also to the unbeliever it can be proclaimed only in this way that it is already here and that on the basis of the perfect tense the future will occur. In this way the preaching of the Kingdom becomes an eschatological entity and a serious responsibility, because a refusal to accept the Kingdom is at the same time a denial of the event of salvation. Thus the proclamation in this case becomes a judgment and provokes further judgment.

10. The Kingdom as Decision

If this were not the case, then the Lord and His apostles could not have made the Kingdom the content of their proclamation. Jesus takes up the proclamation of John the Baptist and commends it to his disciples. He does this in view of the goal of His sending and redemption. In the New Testament therefore the same expressions are used to speak of the proclamation of the Kingdom as for the proclamation of salvation. The proclamation of the Gospel is the news of the King's reign (Matt. 4:23; 9:35). He who proclaims Jesus preaches

31

the Kingdom (Acts 8:12). Paul therefore can call himself only a proclaimer of the Kingdom (Acts 20:25). Through preaching, the King's reign gains realistic presence. "For the faith which responds to the proclamation and acknowledges its witness the perfect tense of salvation, the salvation event as history, becomes the present in the proclamation. It becomes the present tense also in the Sacrament. It becomes a present perfect through the Holy Ghost, who brings and fulfills both methods of confrontation." [19]

Since the kingdom of God is different from the dominion of the world and the latter is to be vanquished by the former, the proclamation forces a decision. "Jesus does not content Himself with a defense against the demonic attack. He takes the offensive. Therefore the concept of kingdom in the words of the Lord has a pronounced polemical accent." [20] Jesus declares war on the demons and the demonic powers and wants to overcome them. He wants to rescue man from their grasp. This occurs when through the preachment He leads his own to participate in the battle, frees from the other kingdom those to whom he speaks and through repentance sends them into the fray. Man must realize that he is bound to the other kingdom and must loosen those bonds with the power of Christ. He is called into the Kingdom to leave the other kingdom. No one can become obedient to the kingdom of God without turning about, repenting, and letting the royal rule of Christ work on him.

The gifts of the rule are described in the beatitudes. Repentance manifests itself in the desire for the treasure (Matt. 13:44 ff.), in the break with the past and with one's surroundings (Luke 9:62). The μετάνοια therefore embraces all of life

[19] H. D. Wendland, *Der Herr der Zeiten* (Gütersloh: C. Bertelsmann, 1936), p. 20.

[20] Ethelbert Stauffer, *New Testament Theology*, trans. John Marsh (New York: Macmillan, 1956), p. 20.

and gives it such a form that something of the kingdom of God already becomes plain in the life of him who is called to the Kingdom. For this kingdom of God is the life which God gives. "μετάνοια is the call to recognize that everything outside of the kingdom of God is dead. It is the radical renunciation of autonomous management of one's life and the turning to the different quality of the life from God. If sin as separation of man from God is death, then a presupposition of life is the conquest of sin through forgiveness. The kingdom of God can have a beginning only where there is forgiveness." [21] Through repentance wrought by the preaching of the royal rule the Kingdom operates among men in this way that they seek forgiveness and are allowed to find it through Jesus Christ. When these presuppositions are present, then only may we speak of a realization of the Kingdom.

Jesus never bestows the gifts of His kingdom by complementing or sublimating human things but only by giving to man a new relationship to the surrounding world and a new goal of life by means of a new life which He has provided through repentance and justification. From this then grows the service which God wants to render the world through His followers and which works itself out in this way that all areas of life are penetrated and renewed by Christ. To give men the gifts of the Kingdom apart from the new life would be tantamount to giving those gifts into the hands of men who are still subject to the other kingdom. If this is not borne in mind, the activity of the church and the mission ever and again leads only to this that the kingdom of God is lost in sinful man's lust for power.

11. The Universality of Salvation

With its fullness of divine gifts this kingdom of God does not now belong to any specified group of men. It is intended

[21] W. Künneth, p. 109.

for all men, also the heathen. If this were not the case, we could not speak of a reign of God, and the kingdom of God could not be the opposite of the kingdom of the world, which likewise demonstrates universality, unity, and closed ranks. In His readiness to save and rescue all men, He proves Himself to be God and Lord of all men. This has not always been recognized in theology. In the Old Testament the reign of God is a theocracy. In Israel Jahweh proves Himself glorious. In the New Testament Jesus comes forward as the Son of David, that is, in the sense of the prophecy of Nathan (2 Sam. 7:12 ff.), as the legitimate successor to claim his throne. He leaves no doubt that Israel is under the very special guidance of God. In the plan of salvation Israel has a special place. Among the nations Israel is the congregation of God which has become the center of the world of nations, so that the heathen may join it and through Israel learn to know the one God and the true worship of God. This was the call of Israel, the meaning of its election. In and through Israel, therefore, the Kingdom became apparent so that it could be bestowed on the other nations.[22]

Therefore Jesus declared to this people that it had a claim on God not as a chosen nation, but only as the congregation of God and only to the extent that its individual members submit to the will of God.[23] Birth does not guarantee membership in the congregation of God and in the reign of God; only he can enter the Kingdom whose righteousness corresponds to that of the Kingdom (Matt. 5:20; 7:13 f., 21). God's rule is bestowed on Israel because He has elected it, but whether it receives a share in the Kingdom depends entirely on whether it accepts the offer of God. God everywhere rejects claims of privilege. He does not surrender His kingdom

[22] J. Jeremias, *Jesus' Promise to the Nations*, trans. S. H. Hooke (Naperville, Ill.: Alec R. Allenson, Inc., 1958), pp. 55 ff.

[23] Holsten, pp. 75 f.

to Israel. In its self-assertion as a nation, Israel decided against Jesus and thus against the Kingdom. By contrast, Jesus praises individual heathen and promises them a share in the Kingdom (Mark 5:1 ff.; 7:24 ff.; Matt. 8:5 ff.; Luke 7:11 ff.). Salvation is not taken away from Israel. It is always first offered to Israel, but from there it goes to the heathen. Mission work among the heathen becomes a sign of the last times.[24]

Although Israel declines salvation, sacrifices the Kingdom, and must be rejected by God, Jesus nevertheless considers Himself the legitimate Bearer of the Kingdom. It also becomes clear in the example of Israel that as representative of the Kingdom Jesus belongs to all men, that God withdraws His kingdom from all human wishful thinking, acts contrary to the human lust for power, excludes all self-salvation, and connects redemption with the last times. The Kingdom is eschatological although it has begun in this time. The next aeon has already begun with it although the aeon of this world has not yet ended.[25] Thus Jesus exercises His royal rule in this world as representative of God's rule over the new aeon. (Matt. 13:41)

During His royal rule the partners in the Kingdom will sit at His table and thus experience the greatest advantage which a king can bestow, while those who thought that they could assert their claim to this kingdom will be expelled. The refusal by Israel and its rejection by God is now the reason why the Kingdom goes to the heathen and creates for itself among them the immediate congregation of God. The Book of Acts illustrates this in a remarkable way. Always salvation is, first of all, offered to the Jews. Thus their prerogative is acknowledged. But, again, their hostility and their blunder

[24] Jeremias, pp. 46 ff.

[25] Oscar Cullmann, *Christus und die Zeit* (Zurich: Zollikon, 1946), pp. 70 ff.

is always the reason why salvation is proclaimed to the heathen (Rom. 11:11). Of course they receive salvation as those who only by the mercy of God have a part in the salvation first intended for Israel. There is therefore no special kingdom for the heathen. God began His kingdom with His own people. Therefore the heathen can only be added, grafted as wild branches into the olive tree. That is why the New Testament church is not suspended in the air, does not stand out of context with the history of salvation, but is linked to the historical saving activity of God. For both Luke in the Book of Acts and Paul in his epistles are at great pains to prove that the people of God coming out of the heathen stand in close connection with the ancient people of God and that this connection agrees with the will of God and with His revelation.

The election of the heathen in the last days also has its special purpose. They are to bring this salvation in Jesus Christ back to the Jews, so that at the end all humanity hears the proclamation of the Kingdom. In the last analysis the mission to the heathen is concerned with the winning of Israel. Its renewed reception is one of the signs of the last times (Rom. 11:11 ff.). Schlier is therefore right when he maintains: "According to these statements the mission to the heathen takes place during the time between the fall and rising again of Israel." [26]

Before we continue to fix the place of the mission to the heathen in the history of salvation, we must remind ourselves of its concrete presuppositions within the history of salvation. God proclaims himself as the Lord of all mankind in the rejection of Israel. The divine character of His reign becomes clear particularly when it puts away all exclusivism and seeks to embrace all men. God does this in order to lead into gen-

[26] H. Schlier, "Die Entscheidung für die Heidenmission in der Urchristenzeit," *Evangelische Missionszeitschrift,* 1942.

uine relationship with Him and His congregation all those who by creation and through His worldwide rule belong to Him. God thus no longer binds Himself to any nation. To do otherwise would contradict the sending of His Son. Christ's redemptive death and resurrection would prove meaningless for the world, and the mission to the heathen would have no basis.

Death and resurrection, however, are the presuppositions of the proclamation of the Gospel of salvation for all people, and this begins with His exaltation. This becomes clear in a statement like John 12:23. Jesus reads His glorification in the arrival of the Greeks. But he also knows that this can become reality only when the seed falls into the ground and dies. Not until his redemptive death has been achieved is His Gospel message for all nations. Through Christ's death and resurrection the message of the Kingdom receives a cosmic significance. Now it is the message for all men. (John 3:16; 2 Cor. 5:18,21; Col. 1:20)

If there were no salvation event, the message about Jesus would probably still produce a good code of ethics but it would not be Gospel for all men and would not be able to answer their needs. But now the message is filled with the salvation event, with forgiveness of sins, and everlasting life. All who allow themselves to be called into the Kingdom can now take comfort and rejoice in this news. The church is the bearer but not the master of this message addressed to all men. She can place herself at the service of the Kingdom but dare not place limits upon it.

12. Did Jesus Want Missions to the Heathen?

Two series of questions arise concerning the problem of the Jews and the heathen. These questions have again and again played a large role in connection with the founding of the mission and even today assert their weight. On the one hand they misled Gustav Warneck to imagine that Jesus had thought in an evolutionistic fashion; Jesus supposedly restricted Himself at first to Israel but later ordered the mission among the heathen. On the other hand the question of whether Jesus wanted the mission to the heathen has never come to rest since Adolph v. Harnack. Today it is still answered in the negative by several exegetes, for instance, by Jeremias. He believes that Jesus still stood in the Old Testament Zion-Jerusalem tradition: that the heathen must come to Jerusalem and as a consequence the mission to the heathen must immediately precede the coming of Jesus. According to this the mission to the heathen in the full sense would first be possible at the coming of the Lord, if at the sudden appearance of the Kingdom Jesus Christ Himself leads the fullness of the heathen into it.

These thoughts were already supported by Zinzendorf and Fr. Fabri and led to this that the modern mission to the heathen was viewed only as preparatory work with the purpose of winning individuals who had been prepared by the Holy Ghost. This led to emphasis on individual conversions because the nations as such were presumably through God's election not ripe for the mission to the heathen. However, the work of both men demonstrates that they as little as those mentioned above doubted that the inner urge of the Gospel presses toward the mission to the heathen and that the early church was led to the mission to the heathen through the gift of the Holy Ghost. The mission to the nations would be legitimate even if Jesus had not given the Great Commission. The horizon of the Gospel is the entire human race. But this does not say that the Lord Himself thought of the mission to the heathen during His earthly life.

For a negative answer to the question some weighty quotations can be adduced on the basis of the New Testament,[27] e. g., Matt. 15:24; 15:26; 10:5 ff.; 10:23. According to H. Schlier, Jesus lived in the immediate expectation of the last judgment and believed that he would not complete his task with Israel before it arrived. The mission to the heathen is said to have come into existence when the resurrection of Jesus, the gift of the Holy Spirit, and the continued deferral of the end of the world made room for the mission to the heathen and supplied the presuppositions for it.

The question remains whether these quotations must necessarily be interpreted in this way or whether they do not rather express a practical concern. Jesus' restriction to Israel may very well have been a temporary self-restriction of His saving endeavor for the sake of the ultimate reception of His message by all men. If it is to become effective, it must be concretized in a congregation. There must be a congregation which believes the Gospel, watches over it, and guards it so that it cannot be misused by mankind. The Gospel has to strike roots before it can grow into a tree. It is not a parasite which attaches itself everywhere and anywhere and sucks itself full. Rather it must first of all be independent and exclusive before it can become worldwide. If Jesus, as Warneck assumed, was still caught up in particularism, then one ought not to say this word in the same breath with world Redeemer. If Jesus had a practical concern in mind, then particularity was the presupposition of universality. In any case, Jesus was not a world evangelist who by his proclamation put the Gospel at the disposal of the heathen without urging them to make a decision.

The worldwide movement of syncretism makes it obvious how the Gospel, given into the hands of the heathen through a wrong method of operation, can be misused when no guardian congregation stands behind it as a clear demonstration

[27] Jeremias, pp. 11 ff.

of the Gospel in life and thought. Already the apostles, to their terror, had to experience the misinterpretation of the Gospel. The Book of Acts provides us with three examples on this point: Simon Magus (Acts 8), the deification of men at Lystra (ch. 14), and those who practiced sorcery in the name of Jesus (ch. 19). In his letters Paul already came to grips with syncretistic tendencies. Thus Jesus had to create a congregation for Himself in which the Gospel could be realized in a manner appropriate to the Kingdom. Might not this be the reason why He restricted his activity to Israel? Jeremias demonstrates that Jesus took a very special position toward the heathen.[28] Lohmeyer also makes this clear. "The problem of the heathen has an immovable place in the message of Jesus (Matt. 8:11; 21:43; 36:28). The goal that the nations should become 'sons of the Kingdom' is clearly expressed."[29] Nevertheless, on the basis of this conception one will have to say that Jesus permitted the mission to the heathen only after His resurrection when Israel had rejected Him.

The transition to the mission to the heathen was no act of desperation but, viewed eschatologically, the rejection of Israel had to serve the purpose of making Jesus the Redeemer of mankind. By means of the saving acts the presuppositions of the universality of salvation are first supplied. Through the resurrection and the exaltation Jesus becomes the Kyrios (Acts 2:36). "Through His resurrection from the dead, Jesus, formerly the Messiah of the Jews, had been enthroned as Lord and Savior of the whole world (Rom. 1:11 f.)."[30] Jesus thus becomes the Lord over the entire creation and simultaneously over that other kingdom, which he has already

[28] Ibid., pp. 40 ff.

[29] Lohmeyer, p. 33.

[30] Anton Fridrichsen, *The Apostle and His Message* (Uppsala: Lundequistaka, 1947).

proleptically conquered (Col. 1:13). The Kyrios of Israel and the Kyrios of the world is now one and the same and thus the contradiction between Matt. 15:24 and Matt. 28:18 ff. is eliminated. On this point Liechtenhan says: "The sending out is a once-for-all act (Luke 10:17-20). Therefore one can draw no further conclusion from the restriction to the lost sheep of Israel. The purpose is to enlarge the little flock." [31] Schlier says it even more pregnantly: "Through the resurrection the missionary commission of the resurrected One legitimately cancels His prohibition against going to the heathen, and this prohibition is the legitimate preliminary step to His missionary commission." [32]

13. The Eschatological Place of the Mission to the Heathen

The death and resurrection of Jesus are the presupposition for the mission to the heathen. Thereby the eschatological turning point is reached and the Kingdom crowds toward completion. This kingdom comes into force through the exaltation of Jesus. He assumes the dominion. Therefore the Great Commission Matt. 28:18 is today understood less as a command than as a proclamation of the coming kingdom, the announcement of the ascent of Jesus to the throne, His enthronement.[33] Jesus has become King of the Kingdom and in that role has the message of the Kingdom proclaimed to men so that they might thereby be prepared for His return and be rescued through this preaching.

The mission is always under the sign of the coming Lord.

[31] R. Liechtenhan, *Die urchristliche Mission* (Göttingen: Vandenhoek und Ruprecht, 1946), p. 23.

[32] Schlier, p. 182.

[33] O. Michel, "Menschensohn und Völkerwelt," *Evangelische Missionszeitschrift*, vi, 1941. E. Lohmeyer, pp. 34 ff. J. Jeremias, op. cit. S. Knak, "Neutestamentliche Missionstexte nach neuerer Exegese," *Theologia Viatorum* (1953—54), p. 27.

41

This gives to service in the mission its most profound meaning and its ultimate goal. "If the coming of the Son of Man includes a judgment upon all nations, then it also demands as presupposition that opportunity has been given to all men to appropriate salvation and that thereby they are put into a position of responsibility. The proclamation of the Gospel to all nations is therefore a postulate of eschatology; that is why the 'Must' of eschatological determinism is mentioned." [34]

Through the mission the church must do nothing less than prepare for the arrival of Jesus. The end can only come when the message of the Kingdom is proclaimed to all nations as a sign over them (Matt. 24:14). Therefore the Holy Ghost leads the church step by step into the mission to the heathen as a fact of the last times and thus prepares for the arrival of Jesus. *Missio* is now the activity of the exalted Lord between His ascension and His return. Thus the church has but one assignment: to carry forward the history of salvation through the proclamation of the Perfect One and through the announcement of His kingdom in the gathering of His congregation, "until He comes." [35] A number of Dutch theologians reach important conclusions on the basis of these observations in order to obtain a new understanding of the church and the mission. I will first summarize our observations according to the basic work of Hoekendijk, who at the same time also builds the bridge to the next chapter. [36]

In his fundamental chapter on the context of the mission, Hoekendijk makes clear for us that it not only points to the coming end and the sudden appearance of the Kingdom but that it is itself already a sign of the coming. The command

[34] Liechtenhan, p. 32.

[35] Cullmann, pp. 145 ff.

[36] J. C. Hoekendijk, *Kerk en Volk in de duitse Zendingswetenschap* (n. p.), pp. 223 ff. In addition to Hoekendijk see also W. Freytag, *The Gospel and the Religions* (London: SCM, 1957).

is connected with the apocalyptic signs and woes. So it belongs to the final signals which God gives to men before the end (Mark 13:10; Matt. 24:14). The mission is itself an apocalyptic event. Hoekendijk here adopts the thesis supported by Cullmann,[37] that 2 Thess. 2:6, 7 must be understood with reference to the mission so that the repentance of mankind which has not yet taken place and the still unfinished proclamation of the Gospel among the nations become the restraining factor before the coming of the Lord. That is why the interim period is the expression of God's great patience with mankind.[38]

Viewed in this way the mission receives its significance in the history of salvation. All power in heaven and earth is now given over to the Son of Man (Dan. 7:13, 14; Matt. 28:18). The service of the nations now belongs to His triumph. His glory has begun (Matt. 16:27; 26:62). The messianic promise in Isaiah 2:2 is fulfilled. The faith in Jahweh through the proclamation of the message of the Kingdom embraces all of humanity as it is viewed by Second Isaiah. By means of the proclamation national barriers disappear. All are called to the Kingdom. This era began with the rejection of Israel. But the mission to the heathen is expressly made dependent on the gift of the Spirit (Luke 24:49; Acts 1:8). This is the great event of the end-time.

The Holy Ghost leads to the spiritual apostolate which is

[37] Cullmann, pp. 145 ff.

[38] Commentaries vary widely in interpreting the "restraining force." It refers to the Jewish state (Warfield, Moffatt), the Holy Spirit, a limit of time fixed by divine decree, a personification of traditional supernatural mythology (Neil in the Moffat series), Satan (Bicknell in the Westminster Series and Frame in the ICC Series), law and order as personified at that time in the Roman rulers (Tertullian et al.). The last of these is the most generally accepted. If taken in the sense of "retard" it could refer to the conflict between the mission and the world and point forward to vv. 13 ff. Cf. Cullmann, ibid. (Tr.)

expressly the apostolate to the heathen. Later we will give this idea detailed attention.

On the basis of these statements it becomes clear, we hope, that the church is to be understood only as an eschatological entity and that consequently the mission can be nothing else than a continuation of the history of salvation as the exalted Lord uses His congregation among the nations. The church is the distinguishing mark of the new age in which all believers have a part and which must be proclaimed to all unbelievers, before it passes into fulfillment. All the activity of the church now stands under this distinguishing mark. This activity can only then be correct when in all its ramifications it has as its goal the winning of the unbelievers. The *missio Dei* is achieved in the service which the church renders. It is now necessary to describe the way in which this *missio Dei* is carried out.

[III]

THE SENDING

1. The Meaning of the Sending

THE MISSIO DEI is the work of God through which everything that He has in mind for man's salvation — the complete fullness of His Kingdom of redemption — is offered to men through those whom He has sent, so that men, freed from sin and removed from the other kingdom, can again fully come into His fellowship. Thus the sending becomes an act of the love of God to lost men. It is an expression of His mercy.[1]

This has little in common with the Pietistic motive of compassion for the heathen, which was strongly suffused with the consciousness of Christians being the *beati possidentes*. The object was not alone to bring salvation to man through the Gospel proclamation, but also to snatch them from their moral and earthly depravity and to help them to an existence worthy of a human being.

In order to bring man to salvation, God woos him through His revelation, through His Word. Hence the *missio Dei* is most intimately tied up with revelation. God reveals Himself in that He performs the sending Himself. If there were no *missio Dei*, then we would also have no revelation. He sends His Word to man and reveals Himself in such a way that, in His Son He Himself comes to them through the Holy Ghost. (John 3:16; Rom. 1:16)

[1] G. F. Vicedom, *Die Rechtfertigung als gestaltende Kraft der Mission* (Neuendettelsau: Freimund Verlag, 1952), pp. 9 ff.

45

2. The Sender and the Sent

Through the love of God, which takes form in revelation and is imparted to man in the sending, the God who reveals and sends connects Himself through His Word, His Spirit, and His work with the one who is sent, and through him in turn with those who hear the proclamation. This was worked out by the conference at Whitby,[2] a meeting [3] which in its theological discoveries is still barely recognized.[4] Through the sending God builds the bridge and establishes the connection with men whom He desires to save. Consequently, from God's point of view the sending always has a definite command and concrete goal which has to be attained. This command makes the church and her mission only a connecting link, not an entity for itself nor an independent work. The church does not choose her assignment by herself. Along with her mission she is never merely a necessary arrangement serving man's religious inclination. She is above all not a cultural entity and therefore has no primary cultural assignment. Nor is the church an ecclesiastical-political affair. The mission above all does not have anything to do with a national thrust toward expansion. The church can accomplish a variety of things, but she must not seek these apart from her one real duty. Separated from this duty, all other concerns belong to the other kingdom.

The church and its missions cannot be conceived apart

[2] This was the site of the fourth International Missionary Council Conference. Following Edinburgh (1910), Jerusalem (1928), and Madras (1938), it was held at Whitby, a little town outside of Toronto, Ontario, July 5—24, 1947. (Tr.)

[3] The major literary results of the conference were twofold: J. W. Decker, Norman Goodall, and C. W. Ranson, "Partners in Obedience," *The Witness of a Revolutionary Church* (New York: International Missionary Council, 1947), and K. S. Latourette and Richard Hogg, *Tomorrow Is Here* (New York: Friendship Press, 1947). (Tr.)

[4] W. Freytag, *Der Grosze Auftrag* (n. p., 1948), pp. 32 ff.

from God and can therefore be understood only from the viewpoint of the existence of God and His mission. The former are nothing more than an instrument, a work-schedule of God in relation to His creatures, a gathering of those who permit themselves to be called to Him through God's definite sending. Thus the accent of the church and missions is always on the Sender who wants to accomplish His purposes through them. Thus each sending is in the first instance a declaration about the Sender, the God who exerts Himself for men. (Is. 6:8; Gen. 12:1 ff.)

The words the Scriptures use regarding the sending speak simultaneously about the absoluteness of the will of the One who has given the command. The one who is sent is always the one who by sheer necessity stands under the will of the Sender (1 Cor. 9:16 ff.). The Sender calls to His service the one who is sent. He gives full authority to the one sent because the latter must always act in behalf of the Sender. Thus the mission is spared every caprice and whim, as well as every human or churchly inclination, even though these may be ever so deeply fixed in a particular piety and grounded in a particular theology. "At the outset of the mission always stands God's 'I,' the 'I' which is established in the Holy Scriptures."[5] Thus the ones who were sent can always deliver the message only if they say with the prophets: "Thus saith the Lord!"

3. Election and Sending

The attitude of the church toward the world is determined through the sending. The church must regard herself as the carrier of the message to the world. This was developed among the Dutch in this way that one asked, "What is the position of the people of Israel in the world, and what is

[5] Friso Melzer, *Ihr sollt meine Zeugen sein* (n. p., 1955), p. 7.

47

Israel's attitude toward the heathen?" In the following presentation I follow J. Blauw.[6]

To begin with, God carries out the sending into the world in such a way that He elects for Himself from among the nations the nation that belongs exclusively to Him, and calls and sends it. Israel already had a mission call. It would be a grave misunderstanding to see in the election of Israel only an arbitrary act of the autonomous God, who in His sovereignty leaves all other nations to themselves in order to select a nation and show preference to it. Precisely the election of Israel is a service of God toward the nations. It was part and parcel of His *missio*. Through this election the other nations were also included in His promise (Gen. 12:1 ff.). Israel was for them the bearer of the promise and the mediator of the blessing, lofty sign of the fact that they, too, could be saved and partake of salvation.

> The God to whom the *world* belongs is the God who has chosen His people. . . . The Bible does not begin with the God who elects, but with the God who is the Creator and therefore the God who can elect.[7]

He is the God who *can* elect, and who therefore also *does* elect the heathen.

Therefore, to begin with, God called His people as a whole into service to the heathen of the Old Testament. By the position of His nation among the people of the world, by the faith and obedience of His people, by the dealings of God with them even in their disobedience and apostasy, by all of

[6] Johannes Blauw, *Goden en Mensen* (Groningen: J. Niemeijer, 1950). J. Blauw, a former secretary of the Dutch Missionary Council, Amsterdam, The Netherlands, is now professor of comparative religion at the University of Utrecht.

[7] O. Weber, *Bibelkunde des Alten Testaments* (Tübingen: Furche Verlag, 1947), p. 42. Weber is professor of theology at the University of Göttingen.

these examples it was to become evident to the other nations how God deals in His holiness and love with His people, with men whom He desires to save. At the same time people could realize how the life of a nation could be determined by its faith in God. Thus Israel became at one and the same time a point of attraction as well as a warning to the heathen.

> The stern law of God which separated Israel from the heathen was in force until the day of Jesus Christ in order to frighten the heathen, to hold before them the holiness of God, and to witness to them that one does not become a member of God's people by one's own choice or proper conduct.[8]

God executes the sending in such a manner that He Himself deals with His people and sends men to them who can rule and direct His people in His behalf. Already here the fact becomes clear that since the Fall men are without leadership and go astray (1 Kings 22:17; Is. 13:14; Zech. 10:2). The fellowship of the nations of the world with God is broken, but God leads His people by free grace. That is why He sends His people men who are to lead and rule them.

The same thing is true when Israel asks for a king. It is significant that God indeed permits a kingdom, but first gives it the correct meaning: The king is to be the shepherd who leads the people on God's behalf. Thus the king had a salvatory duty. God is the Shepherd (Psalms 23 and 80). He sends shepherds who lead the people in His stead (Is. 40:11; Jer. 3:15; Ezek. 34:23). Accordingly, Israel is under the special care of God. He gives her every opportunity to remain, of all the nations of the world, the people of God and, through her life and presence, to bear witness to God. She stands beneath God's guidance. This saving will of God, i. e., to lead His people, deeply penetrates even the New Testament (Matt. 9:36; John 10:1; 1 Peter 2:25; Heb. 13:30). For the first, then,

[8] A. DeQuervain, "Der Ewige König," *Theologische Existenz,* LVIII (n. d.), 23.

God carries out the sending in such a way that He serves His people through His guidance.

Israel lived among the nations. She was always in danger of becoming like them. Above all, after the conquest she got acquainted with the gods of the agrarian culture, without whose favor the production of the fruit of the land was unthinkable. The transition from wilderness wandering to fixed residence, from a nomadic life to the tilling of the soil, and finally to the civilizing and cultural upsurge of the time of the kingdom — all of these were not merely technical matters, but predominantly religious. Thus the reception of the new cults and ways of life became a vital question for Israel.

Israel was constantly surrounded by apostasy. For that reason God not only sent His people kings but above all prophets, to whom He made His will known, who ever and again drew the line over against apostasy. The prophets impressed the divine will on the shepherds of the people of God and emphasized the demand and the promise of genuine divine guidance. The separation from the other nations was achieved through the Law. The prophets proclaimed the correct meaning of the Law as well as its correct application. The result was that in spite of much unfaithfulness, Israel could exert an exemplary influence in its environment. By means of this separation from the other nations, the particularism of the salvation of Israel became the presupposition for the fact that salvation became meaningful for others also.

In all this a twofold fact became apparent — important both for the origin of the idea of missions in the Old Testament and as a prelude to what later took place at the time of Jesus: (1) The mission concept grows under the call of repentance and (2) the prophets receive the worldwide vision to the degree that Israel, because of her apostasy, could no longer be called God's people. When Israel regarded herself secure and identified herself with God's rule, she was doomed to perish. At this point there dawns within Israel the understanding of an eschatological salvation and of the magnitude of the church of God among all nations. Passing on salvation to others by the remnant of Israel, hence, by the real church of God in the midst of the people, is now understood as the genuine calling. At this point Jerusalem becomes the center of genuine worship of God and all nations should have part in this salvation.[9]

Thereby, however, God's real goal for Israel is not yet attained and her particular assignment not yet fulfilled. The more the "remnant" recognizes itself as the true Israel, the more its existence points to Him who is to come as the promised Messiah and Redeemer, as the Servant of God, who will bring salvation to all men. Thus Israel remains the people of God in the remnant church, the bearer of the revelation. God likewise identifies Himself with the promises to Israel for the sake of the One who is to come, whom God will give to all men and who will bring them into His fellowship. Israel's mission call was finally fulfilled when God sent His Son as the Son of David — the Son of man — in order to reveal Himself to all men in His love and to accomplish His work of grace for all men.[10]

4. The Special Missio Dei

Hence God Himself does mission work. In His mercy He once more makes Himself the Shepherd and Messenger

[9] J. Hempel, "Die Wurzeln des Missionswillens im Glauben des Alten Testaments," *Zeitschrift für die alttestamentliche Wissenschaft,* LXVI (n. d.), pp. 244 ff. J. Jeremias, *Jesu Verheiszung für die Völker* (Gütersloh: C. Bertelsmann, 1956), pp. 47 ff. The latter has been translated under the title *Jesus' Promise to the Nations* (Naperville, Ill.: Alec R. Allenson, 1958).

[10] O. Cullmann, *Christus und die Zeit* (Zurich: Zollikon, 1946), pp. 99 ff.

of His people languishing in confusion (Matt. 9:36; Mark 6:34). He sends the Servant of God, from whose promises the Old Testament church of God had learned that its God is a God of the nations. He does His mission work through His Son, who Himself becomes an apostle, that is, one who is sent (Heb. 3:1). In Him He makes the salvation intended for all men a reality and calls them anew into His fellowship.

The special *missio Dei* begins with Jesus Christ, for in Him God is both the Sender and the One who is sent, both the Revealer and the Revelation, both the Holy One who punishes and the One who redeems. Through His Son in the incarnation and enthronement God makes Himself the very content of the sending. Through His Son it becomes clear once and for all who God is, what He is, how He works, how He thinks in regard to men, how He redeems them, what salvation He has prepared for them, how men may draw nigh unto Him, and how they are received into His fellowship. That now applies to all men. No one now can seek his own way of salvation. No one can sidestep this Jesus. Everyone must decide about Him and through Him, for in Him the God who is their Lord since creation deals with men.

Thus Jesus has His own mission assignment in this sending, but it is always the assignment and will which the Triune God gave to Himself for the world's salvation. Jesus always acts in harmony with the Father, and He works as if the Father Himself were "on the job." He fulfills the work of the Father (John 4:34) and this is the proof that God has sent Him and that He is at work (John 9:3 ff.). In the sending it should become clear to men that the Father is in the Son and the Son is in the Father. That makes the sending a matter of the utmost seriousness. Through this sending men are placed before the only living God; their former gods are declared nonentities and their ways of salvation false, for He alone is Salvation and He alone brings salvation.

This is possible only because Jesus not only delivers a message, but because He Himself is the content of that message and brings salvation. Thereby salvation is removed from all human speculation and all meditation as well. The One who is sent by God accomplishes salvation on the cross and through the message of the cross gives content to every sending. Through the resurrection He overcomes all the needs of men — needs which always revolve about death — and gives the assurance of everlasting life. Through reconciliation and the bestowal of everlasting life the fellowship with God is perfected and the proclamation concerning it receives its urgency in its eschatological emphasis.

Through the exaltation Jesus becomes Lord over all hostile powers seeking to destroy God's work of salvation, and He becomes Lord also over that other world which comprises the kingdom of darkness. He becomes the Head of His church. Thus God solves all the great central questions which have ever agitated religious people, not as man imagined, but in His own way, and therefore in an absolutely valid manner. Man is lifted out of his self-deification and again made into a creature and "the *vis-a-vis*" of God. With Jesus Christ the time of darkness and ignorance ends. Whoever meets Christ is summoned to a decision and thereby to repentance.

The work of providing the content of the sending is completed in Jesus, and thus meaning and goal have been given to every sending. Beyond Jesus there is no further revelation of God. Even the Holy Ghost derives His message from the things of Jesus and in this way leads men into all truth. Since Jesus died and rose for the salvation of men, any redemption apart from Him is impossible, even though men ever and again strive to classify Christ among many figures who try to indicate a way of salvation. Whoever places Christ's "once-for-all-ness" in question also places the one God who has sent Him in question. Only through the Son do men learn to know this

God and only through Him do they find the way to the Father. Thus Jesus is not only a onetime figure in history, but He is also unique in His design and purpose (Rom. 6:10; Heb. 6 passim; 1 Peter 3:18). On the basis of this fact all attempts of religions and philosophies to replace Him will be doomed; on the basis of Him every effort of syncretism which wants to supplement Him, or embrace Him, or make Him subservient to itself, breaks down. Through Him every self-made redemption by man, be it ever so pious, becomes rebellion against the redemption-will of God and again reveals the fact and the consequences of man's fall into sin.

Men can take Jesus only as He is or they receive no share in Him. They can only take a stand toward His message, submit to it, believe it, and permit themselves to be saved through Him. Jesus' message is exclusive since it is totally bound to the one God. But it is at the same time also universal since it corresponds to the kingdom and government of God, which embraces the whole world (Acts 4:12; John 6:68). The message of Jesus belongs to all men.

Apart from this *missio Dei* in Jesus Christ there can be no further sendings today. Everything that happens since His *missio* has proceeded from Him, has been determined by Him, is encompassed by His sending, and is His continuation of His sending. He is everything that embraces for us the content and purpose of the sending. As all of us have become fellow creatures of Jesus through His incarnation and as we, through His redemption have become brothers (Rom. 8:29; Heb. 2:11) and citizens of His kingdom, so, as those whom He has called into His service, we are mere fellow missionaries and vessels of His sending. In this way the service of the church and the mission in Him remains God's own work.

The mission to the heathen as we have it today is possible only because God continued His sending and through the gift of the Holy Ghost, out of the onetime sending of His Son, made a continuing mission. Now it becomes obvious to all men that God has tied His entire salvation to His Son and also that He does not stop in His attempt to win men by His love. There would be no church, no congregation of God among all nations, and consequently no mission, if God did not Himself thus work among all nations through the gift of the Holy Ghost, as Luther described it in the explanation of the Third Article.

The Holy Ghost is the impulse to missions. The apostles are definitely to begin their work and fulfill their call only after the bestowal of the Spirit (Luke 24:49; Acts 1:8). Through the outpouring of the Spirit they are led to the preaching on Pentecost, to the establishment of the first congregation, and from there, step by step, to the mission. Wherever they go they are driven by the Spirit, and wherever they deliver their message the Spirit is at work with them. Without the gift of the Holy Ghost they would never have found the way to the heathen and as a result the redemption which occurred in Jesus Christ would have remained meaningless for mankind. Possibly a Jewish sect would have come into being, but no church to embrace the nations.

The Holy Ghost, too, is sent (John 14:26; 15:26; 16:7). He proceeds from the Father and the Son; hence in His sending the fullness of the grace of the Triune God is given. Where He works, the Triune God is at work. In Him God, in His relationship to the world, continues His presence among men and imparts to them what has been done for them.

> But between His (Jesus') ascension and return, He is with people in that He will be there in the Holy Ghost. The Holy Ghost is the power through which and in which Christ Jesus, who sits at the right hand of God, is present on earth.[11]

[11] H. Schlier, "Die Entscheidung für die Heidenmission in der Urchristenheit," *Evangelische Missionszeitschrift*, VII (1942), 177, 178.

God is never merciless. Whenever He gives His own a command, He always works along and does not stand to one side like a human boss would in supervising laborers. The Holy Ghost brings the presence of God and the certainty of His presence. The Triune God is present in His Spirit.

The Holy Ghost also is Lord (2 Cor. 3:17). The Kingdom is given in Him, for He Himself is this kingdom in the working of God (Matt. 3:11; John 1:20; 1:27; 1:33; Acts 1:5). Jesus makes His promised presence a reality in Him (Matt. 28:20). Whoever therefore is driven and led by Him has the evidence that God wants to accomplish something special through him either in the congregation or through the congregation in the world. The Spirit is always the co-witness in the proclamation and doctrine (Acts 5:32; 15:28). Through His gift and presence the success of the proclamation is evident, for He is the expression used in Scripture for the efficacy of the Word (Acts 19:2 ff.). In these attributes the Holy Ghost continues the mission which God had begun in His Son Jesus Christ until Jesus Himself will return and terminate the mission. The Holy Ghost does this in such a way that He calls men to faith, leads them to witness, and puts them to work.

5. The Apostles

Up to now we have described the *missio Dei* mainly as a direct activity of God through which He reveals Himself as the One who deals with man and saves him. Since the exaltation of Christ, the Holy Ghost carries out this direct action in such a way that the Holy Ghost makes men His messengers and instruments, and commissions and sends them in the name of Jesus.

Those who were specially called by the Lord and sent out with a definite charge are called apostles in the New Testament. They were chosen by the Lord Himself and equipped with His power of authority. They could not choose their own calling. They often consented only with inner reluctance and had first to be conquered by the Lord. They were always equipped with a definite commission — to proclaim the message of salvation, in order to lead men to faith in the One who gave the mandate to the apostles, and to gather them into the congregation of the Lord. Thus their work is always derived from the *missio Dei*.

We find a double call and commission for the apostles in the New Testament. The Lord Jesus, during His life on earth, selects them from the great multitude of His followers. Therefore they become apostles by a special act of His will and on the basis of a special charge. For this the Lord derived strength in prayer (Mark 6; Matt. 10; Luke 9). Most exegetes today assume that this first selection dealt with a one-time, closely limited sending, with the same commission which the Lord also had to fulfill.[12] Thus they were also empowered by their Lord to do exactly what He Himself did — to undergird and expand His messianic work (Luke 9:2; 10:7-9). Apparently their commissioning was a one-time occurrence because, following their return, we find them keeping close company with the Lord in His work. Thus, they did not have an independent assignment so long as the Lord remained on earth.

As we know, during the ordeal of the Passion the disciples deserted their Lord. Thus after Easter He had to call them together again, equip them anew, explain to them the meaning of what had happened, and call and send them out a second time. This second sending, this time by the resurrected Lord, is final (Matt. 28:19; Luke 24:47 ff.; John 20:21; Mark 16:15). Jesus has forgiven the apostles, restored the former fellowship, and removed all obstacles.

According to His instruction, the proclamation of the

[12] G. Stählin, "Die Endschau Jesu und die Mission," *Evangelische Missionszeitschrift*, XV (1950), pp. 99 ff.

apostles henceforth is nothing else but the interpretation of the historical events of His earthly life, especially those events from His arrest to His ascension.

> God uses His apostles, their commitment and their loyalty, in order to open the eyes of men to this divine act, so that it also happens to them and they place themselves in His service.[13]

For that reason the second sending is no longer modified by space and time, but it leads into the entire world. It is universal in a double sense: to the end of time and to the ends of the earth. Through this mission the Lord lays claim to all of humanity and interprets His saving acts in such a way that they become for each man the determining factor for his salvation.

In both commissionings it is striking that Jesus sends only men although He had many women as followers and even though He uses also women as witnesses to His resurrection. It must also be further asserted that this second commissioning is not synchronized with the outpouring of the Holy Ghost. The former precedes it and thus it can be said that the call to the apostolate was given by the Lord Himself whereas its execution is derived from the Holy Ghost.

> But that means that the apostolate does not derive from the possession of the Spirit given to the church (as important as the Spirit may be for the execution of her mission) but from the mandate of the risen Lord. That is clearly set forth in all sources.[14]

Accordingly the resurrection is the necessary antecedent of the sending, the *conditio sine qua non,* from which the apostles receive their commission. But this commission becomes a reality only through the coming of the Holy Ghost.

[13] R. Liechtenhan, *Die urchristliche Mission* (Göttingen: Vandenhoeck und Ruprecht, 1946), p. 74.

[14] Schlier, p. 179.

From thence (Easter and Pentecost) the apostles first are what they have been designated and commanded to be: carriers of the kerygma. Starting here the church first began to develop from its original form made up of a circle of apostles who believed in the living Lord Jesus Christ into a church which grows and increases in the world.[15]

The installation into the apostolic office and the commissioning are based on the resurrection appearances, since the Risen One on the one hand renews and confirms the apostolic status of His disciples and, on the other hand, establishes it anew, in an entirely new way.[16]

This fact has such a strong impact that in the apostolic preaching it is not the cross, but the resurrection which always occupies the central position. It is the decisive fact. Only when there is resurrection, judgment, and eternal life with God, does the cross take on significance. For that reason, above all, mission work is founded on the resurrection. Without the resurrection Jesus would not be the Redeemer of the world.

Along with the spreading of the message of the resurrection another fact also becomes evident: In the question as to who could call himself an apostle the emphasis is not placed so heavily on the call and commission or on the ability for that call, but rather, that one is a witness to the resurrection. He must be able to witness to the appearances of the risen Savior and thereby also to this decisive fact of redemption (Luke 24:29; Acts 1:22; 1 Cor. 15:8 ff.). Paul, too, could rightfully validate his apostleship only by stating that he had seen the Risen One (1 Cor. 9:1). The apostles must also have been companions of the Lord (Acts 1:21). Thus they are eyewitnesses of historical occurrences, of the life, death, and resurrection of the Lord. Thereby the apostolic

---

[15] K. Barth, *Kirchliche Dogmatik* (Munich: Chr. Kaiser Verlag), IV, 1 (1953), p. 373.

[16] W. Künneth, *Theologie der Auferstehung* (Munich: Claudius, 1951), p. 79.

message is protected against all spiritualizing. The Christian sermon is therefore the recital of the life of Jesus and is not a popularized explanation of a system of doctrines.

Such a system may have been important, too, but it is always secondary.

> They [the apostles] have been called out by God from among all men as witnesses of God's own work. They can and should declare God before the entire world, that all the world may hear that God has spoken and acted in Jesus Christ and how He has spoken and acted toward His people.[17]

Thus they are witnesses of the work of Jesus. It is decisive, however, in this connection to observe that not all witnesses become apostles, but only those who received a special call and a special mandate. We know that there were many witnesses of the risen Lord, but only twelve are chosen.

It is quite true that the risen Christ called and sent the Twelve. But with equal emphasis we maintain that this was done simultaneously through the Triune God. The apostles were sent also by the Father because Jesus as the Risen One in this act represents the Father and adds the sending of the apostles to His own sending. Thus these are basically not different sendings. It is always the same *missio Dei* which takes place (Matt. 28:18 f.; John 20:21).[18]

6. The Name "Apostle"

The apostles thus occupy a unique and basic position in the church. As witnesses of the life and resurrection of Jesus they are the connecting link between the Lord and His church which no longer knows Him in His bodily presence. There were more witnesses of the earthly life of Jesus, for Jesus had many followers. For that reason other witnesses could also

[17] Barth, I, 2 (1938), p. 913.

[18] Stählin, pp. 97 ff.

be designated as apostles in the early church, e. g., disciples who accompanied the apostles (Acts 14:4, 14). James, the brother of the Lord, is also called an apostle at one place. (Gal. 1:14)

In general, however, the New Testament writers are quite cautious about calling anyone "apostle." Luke shows a certain hesitancy with regard to Paul in this respect. The data persuade us that the church did not feel authorized to call its emissaries apostles. Nor could anyone apply this title to himself. There was no legal claim to this title. When the disciples argued among themselves as to who might reign with Jesus, they were rebuked in their claims by the Lord Himself (Mark 9:38 f.). One can perform deeds in the name of Jesus and also accomplish what Jesus commanded the apostles, but this does not give one the right to use the name "apostle." (Luke 9:49 ff.)

In order to be an apostle one must be personally called and authorized by the Lord Jesus. This becomes particularly evident in the apostle Paul's discussions of his apostolic office. He lays the greatest emphasis on his complete equality with the apostles. He is concerned with the recognition not of his person but his work. For that reason he supplies his proof of having received a special commission for the apostolate to the Gentiles. This is the service to which he has been called and for which he has been set apart while in his mother's womb (Rom. 1:1; Gal. 1:15). He is certain that he has received his office from the Risen One for he himself has seen Him. Thus he is a witness to the resurrection and he is fully aware that this is an incredible and incomprehensible fact (1 Cor. 15:8 ff.). Consequently he claims the same authority and credentials for his office as the other apostles, and these accepted him, though with some hesitation.

However, he declined the proof which was later advanced — namely, the explanation that his experience was ecstatic,

61

(1 Cor. 14:1 ff.). He does not appeal to his visions and experiences (2 Cor. 12:1 ff.). Although they meant much to him, he does not use them as a guarantee of his commission. For him the decisive thing was that the Risen One had appeared to him and that He had dealt with him through Ananias and the church (Acts 9:1 ff.; 22:3-16; 26:9-18). He had seen the Risen One (1 Cor. 9:1). The co-workers of Paul, both Timothy and Apollos, were not honored with the name of "apostle."[19]

The problem which confronts us here has been treated specially by Fridrichsen.[20] He believes that it can be established, on the basis of the previous observations and from Gal. 2:7, that in reality there were only two apostles — Peter for the circumcised and Paul for the uncircumcised; that each presumably was surrounded by a group of helpers over whom he claimed authority on the basis of his special call; that James was the leader of the Jewish church; that Peter therefore proclaimed the resurrection as the fulfillment of the Jewish hope of a Messiah; that Paul proclaimed Jesus as the Lord of the world on the basis of the resurrection; that the work of the Twelve came to an end with the first sending; that after the resurrection they were no longer apostles; that under Peter and Paul the apostolate of the church took shape. And so he thinks that Peter was conscious of his responsibility for the advance of the Gospel among the Jews, even though he did not restrict himself to them, and Paul, on the other hand, for the mission to the Gentiles, although he always began with the Jews; that alongside of these there were numerous other mission endeavors.

He concludes that the apostolic office could be claimed

[19] However, it seems from Acts 14:4, 14 that Barnabas is called an apostle along with St. Paul, although in 9:27 he is by implication distinguished from "the apostles." (Tr.)

[20] Anton Fridrichsen, *The Apostle and His Message* (Uppsala: Lundequistaka, 1947).

only by two but that the work of this office could be carried out by many. Allegedly only the two apostles have final authority. We can leave it an open question whether Fridrichsen has rightly understood the apostolic office. But we accept his other point, namely, that the service of this office can also be performed by others.

7. Apostolic Office and Church

Although Paul had received the authority of the office from the Risen One, he did not question in the least the right of the prophets and teachers in Antioch to commission him. He submitted to the leaders of the church in that place who acted at the behest and under the direction of the Holy Ghost. This action does not occur in this way in the case of the other apostles. Moreover, with the other apostles we do not find the large number of co-workers that Paul gathers about himself working under his authority in the churches or among the Gentiles. It seems that the other apostles were more or less "loners" who chose their own work, if they devoted themselves to the mission at all.

This alone is clear from the Book of Acts, that they were very much concerned to establish a connection between the Old Testament people of God and the people of the New Testament as embodied in the mother church at Jerusalem. On the other hand, Paul regards himself as not only responsible to the other apostles and the mother church, but he also concedes to the church at Antioch the right to instruct him about his work. Thereby he already clearly exhibits the attitude which is later shared by other missionaries in the church. He does his work in the name of the church and the church is responsible along with him for his work. Both are implied in Paul — the apostolic authority and the co-responsibility of the church.

This demonstrates also that Paul alone of those who had

been commissioned by the church could bear the name of apostle (2 Cor. 8:23; Phil. 2:25; Acts 13:1-3). Thus the church could transmit the service of the apostles but could not make anyone an apostle. The apostolic office was not an office of the church. It was unique and basic. The apostles, who were responsible for the polity of the church, did not appoint successors to themselves, but they created a new office for the leadership of the congregation (Acts 14:23; 20:17 ff.). They surrendered the administration of the church and installed, not apostles, but bishops. The authority of the latter can never be equated with that of the apostles.

Thus the office of the apostles is viewed as unique in the church. The apostles have the duty and assignment to establish the church and thereby they become the foundation of the building upon which all other work was to be based (1 Cor. 3:9 ff.; 12:38 ff.). The beginning is always crucial. The successors can only continue to build the way the foundation has been laid, or they must tear down and destroy. The apostles lay the foundation since they are the immediate witnesses of Jesus and can work according to His personal instructions. This gives their work and proclamation the character of revelation. Such a claim cannot be made by the bishops. "Elders and bishops are only watchmen whose concern it is that the building is really continued on the foundation of the apostles. They themselves are not the foundation." [21]

Now the question arises whether there actually is a missionary office in the church. In answer to that question we could refer to the evangelists who were contemporaries of the apostles. But then we must immediately ask the question

[21] O. Cullmann, *Petrus: Jünger — Apostel — Märtyrer: das historische und das theologische Petrusproblem* (Zurich: Zwingli Verlag, 1952), p. 247. This book has been translated by Floyd V. Filson under the title *Peter: Disciple — Apostle — Martyr. A Historical and Theological Study* (Philadelphia: Westminster Press, 1953).

how this office became so solidly grounded. The fact is that the church in every age did mission work and expanded. Thus, in any case, it can be said that the mission does not depend on the transmission of the apostolic office, but on the missionary attitude which the apostolic service awakened and which was transmitted to the church through the apostles. Through the apostolate the church in the time between the two comings of the Lord is called to the task of bringing to all men salvation in Jesus Christ. All ministries of the church are included in this task and it is from this task that they receive point and purpose. This would also be true, even if we had no express mission command.

8. Congregation and Mission — The Apostolate

Not only the existence of the kingdom of God but also the *missio Dei* are evidence for the fact that God deigns to be the God of men and wants to deal with them in His mercy. All of God's saving acts have been for man's sake and intended for him. The report of these deeds is the Gospel which should be preached to all men. Life and salvation of man in the judgment depends on faith in God's saving acts: hence the church has the obligation in the interim between the completion of salvation and the final judgment (when salvation will be revealed as redemption) to call men to repentance and to transmit the saving faith. This she must do until the end of time and world.

In this way the church becomes a pilgrim church which is always on the way to men who as yet do not know salvation. Her service is a "going" from people to people, from continent to continent, and thereby ushers in the day of salvation for the nations.

And so the activity which begins with going and telling is no longer historical, but leads directly to the consummation

65

because of the eschatological authority of Him who now has become Judge and Ruler.[22]

Through the command to conduct missions the exalted Lord transfers the sending to the church and makes her His messenger to the nations of the world. Within the framework of the divine *missio* she is the instrument of God's mercy. He transfers the apostolic function to her. Thus by Him the work of the apostolic office is passed on, bound in its contents to that which the apostles did and preached. This function of the church — its testimony of what God has done for mankind in His kingdom and what He is about to do — has been labeled "the apostolate" particularly by Dutch theologians.[23] We now will attempt to ascertain what this means, and we will later clarify its significance for the work of the church and apply it on the basis of these insights.

In this discussion we follow Hoekendijk in *Kerk en Volk*. He combines the two indicatives of the fulfillment of messianic prophecies (with respect to future prophecy and with respect to historical fulfillment) in such a way that he sees the apostolate indicated in the sending of the Spirit. For him the gift of the Holy Ghost is the presupposition for accomplishing mission work among the heathen. This is the expression of the divine intention, the possibility bestowed by God to turn the promises of the conversion of the world into reality. This becomes a reality in the last days — between the ascension and return of Christ — and therefore is an eschatological act of God by which He carries out His plan of salvation.

These viewpoints already developed previously are implied also in the apostolate. According to 2 Thess. 2:6 f. the mission

22 E. Lohmeyer, "Mir ist gegeben alle Gewalt," *In Memoriam Ernst Lohmeyer*, ed. W. Schmauch (Stuttgart, Evangelisches Verlagswerk 1951), p. 41.

23 A. A. Van Ruler, "Theologie des Apostolats," *Evangelische Missionszeitschrift*, XIX (1954), pp. 1 ff.

is the great postponing power. Through it the world must be prepared for the coming of Christ and for the judgment. Into this purpose of history the mission is injected. The mission has a history-shaping mandate which is given with the apostolate. Therefore the apostolate can only be spoken of in the interim time. With the preceding sendings salvation for mankind had not as yet been provided. Now it is here, and therefore the sending has a universal character and mandate which extends into the goal of all history and into the consummation of the Kingdom.

The apostles are therefore messengers of the last times (Is. 49:8; cf. 2 Cor. 6:1 f.) The apostolate of Paul to the heathen, identical with that to the Jews, has a completely eschatological orientation. The apostle to the Gentiles received his independent status over against the previous commissionings through the gift of the Holy Ghost (Matt. 28:18 ff.; Luke 24:47 ff.; Acts 1:6 ff.; John 20:21 f.). The apostolate and the Spirit are always so related that the former cannot be thought of without the latter. This is true to the extent that Paul actually speaks of the office of the Spirit (John 20:21; 2 Cor. 3:6).

The Spirit leads (cf. John 16:12-15) the apostles into God's plan of salvation, drives them into the work, and shapes it (Acts 16:6; 1 Cor. 9:16). The impulse of the Spirit is so strong that the entire mission is nothing more than a triumphal march of God in whose train Paul follows as a conquered opponent. Thus the apostle becomes entirely God's instrument in His plan of salvation. Christ leads the world through the apostles and thus through the mission to its goal.

In a later work Hoekendijk has condensed and defined this teaching of the apostolate more precisely.

> The Gospel is fulfilled in the apostolate (Rom. 15:19; Col. 1:2). It is brought to its goal. God's battle *with* the world

for the world is waged. The *subject* of the apostolate remains "the apostle" Jesus (Heb. 3:1); the "works of Christ" (Matt. 11:2) are continued in the apostolic "works of the Lord" (1 Cor. 15:58; 16:10). The arena of the apostolate is the world. The content of the apostolate is the lifting up of the banners of salvation, of schalom; the apostolate becomes a reality in the kerygma, the public proclamation of the schalom, in the koinonia, the corporative participation in the schalom, and in the diakonia, the ministering demonstration of schalom.[24]

9. The Theology of the Apostolate

From these principles the Dutch theology of mission seeks to construct a theology of the apostolate in which the eschatological place of mission is essentially retained and the preaching of the Kingdom is designated as *the* task of the church. In order not to make the church the sole mediator of this message, the doctrine of predestination is retained. Through this doctrine one can behold God's immediate relationship to the world and His effect upon the world. Today God Himself is still at work.

The apostolate becomes a mode of expression of the church so that the mission is the threshold where God's immediate activity crosses over to the mediate. God calls through His messengers whom He has prepared for salvation through His predestination. Thus the apostolate and the Spirit are viewed together — the Spirit is understood as the power which always works among men.

At the proper place we will have to resume discussion of the theological inferences to be drawn from these sentences in order to gain the proper understanding of the work of the church.

I would like to insert already at this point that here a revo-

[24] J. C. Hoekendijk, "Die Kirche im Missionsdenken," *Evangelische Missionszeitschrift*, XVII (1952), p. 10.

lution is taking place within theology. The Dutch themselves recognize this.

> If, for example, one places either the Kingdom, the apostolate, or the Spirit in that position which systematics has awarded the church, the result is an earthquake, which makes its eruptions felt even in Christology.[25]

Thus they are aware of the dangers which lie in such a dynamic concept. They realize that they can become too one-sided in eschatology or too predestinarian. They tell us that one must be aware that man can act, for example, in confessing. Thus both the spiritual and the human elements must be retained. Where this takes place even the ethnic and the confessional emphasis in the church can be established from the apostolate.

> But the mission sees more than just nature; it sees history. It sees more than the church; it sees the nations. It sees more than Christology; it sees at least also pneumatology. It knows about the Gospel of the Kingdom, which is not completely identical with the Gospel of Jesus Christ. (He is the Kingdom only in a certain sense, namely, as the incarnation and concealment of the Kingdom.) It understands that the apostle has an office not in the church, but in the Kingdom. It does not only see Jesus Christ and His church, but it sees behind and through them God Himself and His world.[26]

We observe from these quotes that the theology of the apostolate is still in the development process. We also notice the determined effort to arrive at a clear understanding of the various terms in relation to their opposite meanings.

Over against the above we desire first of all to establish what we have found. The sending is, in the first place, not a fact of the last times, but it is based on the operation of the Triune God in His relationship to the world. It receives its

[25] van Ruler, p. 3.

[26] Ibid., p. 5.

eschatological place and urgency through the coming of the Kingdom in Christ Jesus. Again, the sending is not only linked with the gift of the Holy Ghost. We can with equal cogency show that it is based on the completion of the facts of salvation in the resurrection. But it is through the sending of the Spirit that it receives its special power, its full authority, and through the Spirit is linked with the *missio Dei*.

The commission is an objectively established fact founded in revelation and is not dependent on the personal experience of the Spirit. Through this command the church gets its direction which indeed it cannot follow without the Spirit. Thus the apostolate and the Holy Ghost can belong together only with respect to the *execution* of the sending so that the church is preserved from the stagnation of "churchianity."

It is the Holy Ghost who continually keeps alive the commission of the church. He calls men to the ministry of the apostolate and is the equipment for this ministry in which the gift becomes apparent wherever man obeys the mission command. As equipment for the work, as a share in the participation of God's plan, the Holy Ghost gives the ability needed for the apostolate and, through messengers on earth, gathers the church which confesses her Lord until He comes. Through the mandate of the exalted Lord and through the cooperation of the Holy Ghost the church receives her apostolic character and becomes an entity active by her very existence as well as through the special sending.

10. What Does "Apostolic" Mean?

Karl Barth explains it in this way:

"Apostolic" means on the one hand: she [the church] exists through the continuing work and word of the apostles, and on the other hand, she exists in that she herself does what the apostles did and by virtue of the nature of their words and deeds continue to do.[27]

27 Barth, op. cit., II, 2 (1942), p. 477.

Here is where our question arises. If this is the way in which our brethren in Holland understand the apostolate, namely, that in it we see the continuing work of the apostles (which can only be an activity of the Holy Ghost), then their teaching is nothing new. Then they are saying nothing more than what Luther taught concerning the universal priesthood of all believers.

> Through faith in Christ's merit we have nothing less than the forgiveness of sins! This was the belief of the fathers, of the prophets, and of all saints since the beginning of the world. Later this was also the teaching and preaching of Christ and the apostles, entrusted to them to carry it into all the world and to spread it abroad. Even for today and until the end of time this is the unanimous understanding and attitude of the entire Christian church.[28]

Accordingly, through her faith in the deeds of salvation and through her confessional attitude the apostolicity of the church is established, regardless where it is carried out, at home or abroad.

This is approximately what G. Warneck expresses in his own way:

> Within Christian life lay a missionary-minded responsibility and spiritual urge which drove simple disciples of the early Christian era to the spreading of the Christian faith. This drive did not stem from a legalistic obedience to the fixed mission command, but from the new spiritual life which made them witnesses for Christ with an immanent urgency.[29]

However, if we understand the apostolate to mean that today the messengers still have all the gifts and functions of the apostles, then we have to reject this on the basis of

[28] Martin Luther, *D. Martin Luthers Werke*, XXI (Weimar: Hermann Boehlaus Nachfolger, 1928), 219.

[29] G. Warneck, *Evangelische Missionslehre* (Gotha: F. A. Perthes, 1897), I, 126.

what we said previously. Because in what follows we will again and again come into contact with the teaching of the apostolate, we must ask ourselves whether we really may apply the term "apostolic" to the church. The Nicene Creed uses "apostolic" to say that the church rests upon the foundation of the apostlets and prophets and accordingly is an apostolic church, and that she can be this only in so far as she is founded on the apostles in her tradition. If we employ this term in a different sense, we first must investigate whether this can be done legitimately. So far the Dutch theologians have not yet produced such proof.

11. The Presupposition of the Apostolate

Since the apostolic office is given only once we ask what prerequisites are required to carry out the missionary command so that the Holy Ghost through witnesses and messengers can declare the Gospel to the non-Christians and thus bring into being the apostolate of the church. The answer usually is given somewhat casually, e. g., the church has the command to render this service of witnessing. Granted! But this raises the other question: Why is it then that this assignment is so hard for the church to understand and why is it that she feels so little authorization to do her work? As a matter of fact, history shows this has always been the case. God has had to wring missionary service from His church. Why is there so little reference even in our theology to the authorization and impetus for witnessing?

Is not the reason that the church and her theologians have understood too little of the purpose of the Gospel and therefore also have no unified program for the church's work? Is it not true that she knows too little about the prerequisites for the service of witnessing, including the apostolate and the ministry of the apostles? Do we not exhaust ourselves in exploring the fundamentals of the Gospel, arranging our findings systematically, and being content with what we know instead of working out a definite relationship of the Lord to His own, and explaining their ministry.

Only he can become a witness who has met the prerequisites as they were given in the case of the apostles. The latter were taken from the circle of disciples, thus from a group of people who were in fellowship with the Lord and were shareholders in the Kingdom. These disciples all had the qualifications and potentials for apostolic service even though the Lord elected only a few of them to the office of apostle. The discipleship, following Jesus, was still the prerequisite for their call and commissioning. This prerequisite for apostolic service remains. Only he can be a witness who stands in a disciple relationship with Jesus. Where this is the case the urge to witness and therewith apostolic service come spontaneously.

It is a prerequisite to the apostolate and to missionary service, therefore, that the Lord create for Himself a congregation of believers. This congregation always precedes the mission of the church and takes over the apostolic attitude. Thus the mission is not only an event which proceeds from the Spirit. It has a basis on earth in the company of disciples which Jesus still gathers today and which becomes the carrier of the mission. A church can therefore undertake missionary service only insofar as that discipleship exists in her midst. You have to be a disciple before you can be a witness for Jesus.

12. The Discipleship

In the discipleship of Jesus something fundamentally new has come to this world. It is something new also in the history of salvation, for discipleship exists only since and through Jesus. What was labeled discipleship in the Hellenistic world does not correspond to what Jesus brought. In the former it was left to the discretion of the pupil to look for the master, to honor him, to imitate him, and if possible, to surpass him. This was similar to the rabbinical system. What we could call discipleship in the world of religions does not deserve the name because even the most pious saint strives to attain his own ideal of salvation.

If there is no discipleship in the Old Testament, this is due to the fact that it is always combined with the act of following. God could not present Himself as an example in the old covenant. Also, He did not call individuals but a people, and individuals only because they belonged to these people. These people were simultaneously to be His congregation, the holy people of God. All the people were to keep the Law and show themselves to the world as belonging to God. Through this way of life, which was tied intimately to God's will and deeds, they were to transmit what was secured from God to the individual members and thus also communicate it to the world round about.

The New Testament annuls this principle that congenital fellowship is the same as fellowship in salvation. The congregation of the elect comes into existence in this way that Jesus calls men to follow Him. Thus Jesus for the first time gave discipleship its true content; since then there is no discipleship without personal following. By calling the disciples to follow Him the Lord has made Himself the center of this life of discipleship and has built it into a fellowship which He permeates.

The new feature of this discipleship is that one is called into it only by Jesus Himself. The call was first issued by Him personally; later it came through His apostles. The preaching of the Kingdom is always simultaneously a call to discipleship. The *missio Dei* has no other purpose than to make disciples. Basically this also applies to the service of the church, even to the folk church; for every church in one way or another becomes a folk church *(Volkskirche)*, unless it were not to claim membership in the congregation for its children.

It is absolutely necessary for every church that those born into the church should also be counted as belonging to it. Now, of course, no one can become a disciple because his parents decided for him to make use of infant baptism. That was only the first step. Each person will be confronted with a personal decision since the church continually proclaims the call and seeks to lead the one to whom it has been spoken into a personal relationship with the Lord. The initiative for the call always lies with the caller. I cannot become a disciple because I might like to, but because God speaks to me. Where the wish arises, it always originates from being spoken to by God so that an answer must follow. Thus the disciples in the New Testament were called to follow Him. (Mark 1:17; Matt. 4:19; Mark 2:4; 10:21; John 1:35 ff.)

The same is basically true of the larger circle of Jesus' followers whom He addressed in His preaching and attracted by His actions. They, too, could not enroll as His followers on their own initiative (John 15:16). This becomes very evident in the case of the one healed of possession by a devil (Mark 5:18 ff.) who was sent home by Jesus, or of the three followers (Luke 9:57 ff.) to whom Jesus gave such strict conditions that they refused to follow Him.

Whoever commits himself to discipleship must break away from his own ideal of life, for in it only the life of the Master counts — thus, total surrender. Hence Jesus demands at the very outset a break with all former ties. His followers should be completely at His disposal and should listen to no other voice. Even clearer than in the case of the three followers we hear this in the words which practically set aside the Fourth Commandment (Matt. 10:37; Luke 14:26). At this point all other ties must fade into insignificance, even such

75

as are respectful and require filial love. The disciple should without reservation belong to the Lord.

The call to discipleship dissolves former affiliations for these men and turns them over to the Lord. Jesus will be their *Kyrios* (Matt. 24:45 ff.; 25:14 ff.; Luke 12:35 ff.; 42 ff.). The disciples are received as servants and should subordinate themselves to their Lord. For hearing, obeying, and keeping His Word (John 8:31) is the essence of discipleship. As disciples they are so dependent on the Lord that apart from Him they cannot exist. In all matters they are directed by Him and permeated with His very being. Apart from Him they are nothing; with Him and through Him they are everything (John 15). Hence they must be on their guard that nothing draws them away from the Lord or places them in opposition to Jesus, even if they suffer because of this attitude or are misunderstood and hated because of it. (Matt. 10:17 ff.)

Their life is so intimately and existentially bound up with that of their Master that personally they can travel no other way than that which their Master traveled before (John 15:18; 16:1 ff.). That would be impossible if also this very life, which appears to the average man as unjustified and difficult, were not a gift of the Master. Jesus gives them everything that qualifies them for discipleship. In His fellowship He imparts His life to them. (John 14:4), and therewith also His power. Whatever they have surrendered *for His sake* He replaces many times so that they experience no loss and consider themselves richly blessed by Him. Thus they can serve Him unreservedly. (Matt. 19:29)

These disciples underwent the same change through the death of their Lord as is reported to us of the apostles. To begin with, they, too, looked for the earthly goal — the restoration of the kingdom of Israel. Through the resurrection they first grasped the significance of discipleship (John 2:21 f.; Luke 22:38). They must also be gathered anew by the Risen

One and so, through the resurrection, the first congregation comes into being (Luke 24:36 ff.; John 20:24 ff.; Matt. 28:17). Clearly, discipleship involves not only a break with one's environment, but a conversion of the heart (Matt. 19:28; John 3:5), a regeneration to a new Christ-given life, so that with discipleship man also internally appropriates the goals of Jesus. Discipleship thus always claims the total man and has the new man as its goal.

From among these disciples the Lord selected His apostles and sent them out into the world for service. Thus the prerequisite for the call as an apostle was to be and remain a disciple. Not every disciple was called as an apostle. But every apostle was a disciple, and every disciple is a witness of his Lord to whom he is completely committed.

13. Discipleship and Apostolate

The question now arises whether the name "disciple" and what we have said about the discipleship can also automatically be applied to Christians, and whether the prerequisites for the apostolate are thereby supplied. Christians bore various designations in early Christianity. They were usually referred to as those who had come to faith, who possessed the way, namely, those who knew of salvation and the course of the kingdom of God. In both expressions it is implied that these people are in personal contact with the Lord and have personally accepted what Jesus has done for them. But in many places the believers are also called disciples while the apostles are also referred to as the Eleven.

Thus the name "disciple" for the followers of Jesus is also applied in a general way to the Christians who were brought to faith through the work of the apostles. They do not regard themselves thereby as pupils of the apostles but as followers of the Lord whom the apostles proclaimed (Acts 1:15; 6:1, 7; 9:19; 11:26; 11:29; 13:52; 15:10; 16:1 and elsewhere). The name is still applied later to Christians, and above all, to martyrs.[30] That is very significant. Thus also such Christians are called disciples who did not personally know Jesus, to whom the distinguishing marks in the case of the apostles need not apply.

Consequently also the apostles, the witnesses, can call men into the fellowship; and what was said before concerning the disciples of Jesus is also true of Christians. Jesus' servants stand and act in the place of their Lord. They are the mediators of the discipleship. They call people into the fellowship (1 Thess. 1:6; 2:14; Phil. 3:17).

These disciples are certainly no apostles, but they should and may exercise apostolic functions. For that reason they are called to participate in their work of witnessing. As a matter of fact, already at the time of the apostles we find a large number of such assisting co-workers entirely irrespective of the fact that the congregation through their presence witnessed to the death and resurrection of Jesus (1 Cor. 11:26; 15:3 ff.). Each of these disciples is equipped by His Lord with gifts which he needs for his discipleship. Paul describes the Christian in such indicatives that we can only stand in amazement. They have the gifts which they need for their service in the world. They can live in the world only in such a way that they remain in the fellowship (John 17:13 ff.). They, too, have received the mission command and should therefore be co-workers in the kingdom of God. (Col. 4:11)

E. Lohmeyer [31] examines the term discipleship more thoroughly than anyone else. He places the gathering of the disciples in Galilee and lets the missionary command be issued there, not in a resurrection appearance, but by the Lord who

---

[30] K. H. Rengstorff, μαθητής, *Theologisches Wörterbuch zum Neuen Testament*, ed. Gerhard Kittel, IV (Stuttgart: W. Kohlhammer Verlag, 1942), 417—464.

[31] Lohmeyer, op. cit., pp. 22 ff.

reveals to His disciples how His kingdom shall proceed. He views the disciples as the continuation of the Old Testament people of God and interprets this people's existence as purely eschatological.

> They see themselves as God's flock of the last days, as it were, as the true Israel, and are open to the world mission, living on the holy past of the people of Israel and for that reason committed to the immanent and holy future with the Lord.[32]

Accordingly they have received the missionary command as disciples and not as apostles. For that reason all disciples are likewise called to the extension of the Kingdom.

> "Thus, to be a disciple means to become a messenger to all people. They become such not by their own power, but in His name and through the power of His kingdom." [33]

Herewith Lohmeyer has unintentionally supplied to the church the proof for the apostolate. Thus we rightfully assert that the disciples are to fulfill apostolic functions. Thereby the apostolate also belongs to the distinguishing marks of genuine discipleship. Whoever allows himself to be put into the work of spreading the Gospel is a disciple. He bears the fruit which the Lord expects of him.

In order to do the work, the Lord also equips the disciples with the gift of the Holy Ghost. The Holy Ghost gives testimony of Jesus Christ and promotes the mission through this testimony (John 15:26 f.). He turns the disciple into a missionary (Acts 9:17). In the midst of persecution the Spirit fills the disciples with joy (Acts 13:52) and gives him the courage to speak joyfully even under these circumstances (Acts 4:31). The Spirit speaks and works in Jesus' place.

[32] Lohmeyer, "Mir ist gegeben alle Gewalt," *In Memoriam Ernst Lohmeyer,* p. 49.

[33] Ibid., p. 38.

Because of this gift a disciple cannot but join in spreading the Word abroad.

14. The Ministry of the Discipleship

Through the Spirit, then, the disciples become the Lord's witnesses and co-workers. They are to make the people whom they evangelize into what they themselves have become.

Admittedly, that is a very debatable sentence. We know there are no carbon copies in the kingdom of God. Up until now we have been careful not to make missions a subject of propaganda since the essence of propaganda is to re-make people in our own image. However, that only applies to the transmission of the church tradition and to culturally conditioned traits of Christianity and has no bearing on the true disciple relationship. Every man has the right to draw so near to Jesus that he does not first have to become a Westerner before he can understand Him. But one thing he must always be — a disciple of Jesus. Otherwise he cannot be a witness for Jesus.

Thus our ministry should confer upon him a direct relationship to the Lord.

> The ultimate goal of the message of Christ is not to communicate Jesus' teachings or ethical principles, but to bring men into communion with Jesus Himself, and thus to lead them to the inexhaustible Fountain.[34]

They are to be disciples of the Kingdom of Heaven. (Matt. 13:52)

Therefore we dare not Christianize — which always means to place the people addressed into a society conditioned by tradition. Rather, we are to "missionize," which means to bring men to the Lord so that their lives will be determined by Him (Acts 14:21; Matt. 28:19). We do not want to make Chris-

[34] K. Heim, *Leben aus Glauben* (Berlin: Furche Verlag, 1934), p. 69.

tians, but disciples. When this happens, the disciples will again become witnesses. As witnesses they have received the full measure of that which Jesus gives and cannot but lead people to salvation and place them under their Lord. Where this immediate relationship is replaced by a dependence on the missionary, where the mission is determined by the western image, there are no disciples who become messengers through the dynamic of the Word.

The apostolate of the church is based on this discipleship. Such a discipleship is its native soil. Discipleship as the innermost communion with the Lord — a discipleship which places itself in His service and waits for His nod — is the presupposition for the apostolic ministry of the church. Discipleship cannot simply be equated with church, for in every church nominal members outnumber even the unfaithful disciples. But discipleship is present in the church, and the church will always be an expression of what we have demonstrated to be the marks of discipleship, even though at times in an obscure manner.

However, since the church also includes many hypocrites and in her understanding of people today is influenced much more by the image of man handed down by rationalism than by the Word of God, the question arises whether the church can simply be the bearer of the apostolate. Much of what the apostolate demands of man is declined today not because people do not want to serve God, but because man believes he is entitled to special rights and claims according to which also the ministry of the apostolate is to be carried out. Thus the rebellious nature of man reveals itself in the very nature of the church. Nevertheless, the fact remains that the church must fulfill the apostolic ministry if she is to remain true to her nature and does not want to forsake her eschatological role.

The church must do this through people who permit themselves to be called into actual discipleship and so are willing to be enlisted for the spreading of the Gospel. Thus it ought to be the concern of the church as an institution always to represent those who are willing to enter this ministry. The church must, therefore, always set up certain standards and measure herself according to that church which is posited in discipleship. With this orientation concerning the nature of the church the command to missions will no longer be a special mandate for certain restricted groups, nor a legalistic compulsion for the undecided. Rather, missionary performance will become an expression of life flowing from faith and will be determined by the working of God in the *missio Dei*.

15. The Mission and the Church

The question now arises, How is the mission related to the church? We can offer only a twofold answer.

To begin with, the church herself is the result of the apostolate. The sending which God performed through Jesus Christ and which continues its activity from the time of the apostles up to the present day has led to the formation of the church. If God had not sent His Son, there would be no church, no apostolate, no mission. The fact that Jesus Christ permitted His Word to be proclaimed through men and that men have been called out of the world through the message of redemption is what brought the church into existence.

Thus the church is herself the strongest proof that the Gospel also belongs to the heathen. Consequently we must do mission work not because we possess the Gospel, but rather, we have the Gospel only because it is intended for the heathen. Otherwise we would make ourselves lords of the Gospel and abuse the ministry of reconciliation. Because God wants missions to the heathen, we are the church. But since we are the church from among the heathen, we cannot but be a member of the *missio Dei,* an instrument in the activity of God, a sign that God is leading the world to its ultimate end.

As God continued the works of His Son through the apostles, so He carries forward their activity through the result of their work and prolongs it until He has reached His goal (Matt. 24:14). Thus the church's mission is at the same time the *missio Dei* at the present time, included and formed by *the missio Dei* (Matt. 10:16; Luke 10:1; 9:2; John 17:18). The mission of the church is no independent, arbitrary, optional work of the church. It likewise is not determined by circumstances. Instead, the mission is the work which lays the foundation — in its inception, nature, and mandate it is God's own work. God also remains the One who sends, who leads, and who decides in the mission of the church.

There would be a mission even if we did not have a missionary command. For God always grants to His disciples through the working of the Holy Ghost a faith that is not passive, dumb, simply contemplative, or selfish, but a faith which produces in the Christian a restless concern for the salvation of others, a "living and active thing," a faith which lifts the believer out of his own self-edification and makes him a building stone and a builder. Thus the apostles "could not but speak" (Acts 4:20). But this speaking is always an expression of their certainty of redemption and salvation (Rom. 10:8 ff.). They also preached through their lives (2 Cor. 4:11; 5:15). By faith the disciples constantly stand in the ministry of reconciliation, offering men salvation.

The congregation can do this only because the Holy Ghost furnishes the competence (2 Cor. 3:5 f.). He transmits to the church the urgency to witness and thus constantly leads her out of her complacency. Through the Holy Ghost the church is privileged to act in God's stead even as God sent Himself in His Son. The first example of this is in Acts 13:1-3. The church performs the sending and thereby the *missio Dei* becomes visible to the world. God decides meanwhile who is to do the sending and who is to be sent. This sending is described in Acts 14:26, "where they had first been commended to the grace of God for the task which they had now completed" (Phillips). The final meaning of the sending is that the messengers are placed at the disposal of God for the ministry among the heathen. This means not only that the missionaries find their help, their joy, and their comfort in God, but also that God can make complete men of them. The life of the missionaries is laid completely in the hand of God. There can be no retreat. Just as the disciples enter into the ministry of the Lord with everything that they are, so they can now be commended to the Lord.

All this we can clearly see in the life of the apostle Paul. For him there was no sidestepping. He must, "whether it be through life or through his death, praise Jesus Christ with his body" (Phil. 1:20). Even the congregation could no longer recall these messengers. It had to leave them to the grace of God. How seriously this is meant we gather from the fact that we hardly know the exact circumstances of the death of even one apostle. The life of most of them vanishes into the darkness. They were in the grace of God, and that was sufficient.

Today man regards *himself* as responsible and accountable for his life, and therefore he does not concede to the Lord of life and of the ministry that He use his life until death. The will of God, the purpose of the sending, the course of the kingdom of God are no longer considered decisive, but rather the well-being of the messengers, the security of their lives, and their financial backing. If these are no longer guaranteed, the sending comes to a halt, as if the individual or congregation could decide concerning the *missio Dei.* In situations which demand the ultimate sacrifice today, one has to ask himself whether God can still carry out His mission if the rules are to be dictated by such a human view.

16. Church and Apostolate

Here we must once again ask: What place does the church have within this conception of the apostolate? Hoekendijk's reply is radical.

> Where does the church stand in this framework? Certainly not at either extreme or end. In a somewhat exaggerated way we could say: The church *stands* nowhere; she unfolds herself; she happens; she develops as the Gospel of the Kingdom is delivered to the world. The church is only in the act of Christ, that is, in the act of the apostles. Therefore the church has no designated place but is a temporary home, a settlement which never really becomes a home, headed outward toward the ends of the world and forward to the ends of time. The church remains firmly established on the foundation of the apostles and prophets only as long as she goes along with the apostles, that is, to advertise the Kingdom. . . . To bear testimony of the Kingdom to the world is her real work *(opus proprium);* but it is not really *her* work, but the work of the Lord, ἔργον κυρίου. To the extent that the church has part in this work – the apostolate – she is "the church."[35]

Much as we can subscribe to this last sentence, we still have the feeling, that from the viewpoint of this concept not only the whole past thinking of the church is called into question, but also the church is dissolved into an event, into an insensible entity, vanishing continually in the apostolate.

Thus visibility is discarded, for which a man like Bonhoeffer [36] comes out so passionately. So also that is rejected, which we have noted in the foregoing as discipleship, which appears not only in the fellowship, but also in the sending. Dare the nature of the church be described in this manner?

[35] Hoekendijk, *Kerk en Volk in de duitse Zendingswetenschap,* pp. 10—11.

[36] Dietrich Bonhoeffer, *Die Nachfolge* (Munich: Chr. Kaiser Verlag, 1952), p. 66. (English: *The Cost of Discipleship* [New York: The Macmillan Company, 1959], p. 106.)

Obviously the church, also according to the Augsburg Confession, Article VII,[37] is not an institution. However, if the Word is to be properly proclaimed and the sacraments are to be administered according to their institution, a congregation must emerge, an office must be present. Is the church not much more than the apostolate? Even if we restrict her to those who truly believe, even if we apply the term discipleship to her with all rigor, the church nevertheless is more than sending and kerygma.

Certainly the Lord present in His activity must be everything. But where the Lord is, there a visible congregation comes into being and lives [38] not only in the proclamation, but above all in the hearing, which is the prerequisite for the witnessing. The church also lives in the love which through Christ becomes effective in her precisely through the hearing. She lives in adoration and doxology. She lives in the Sacrament and thereby in fellowship with her exalted Lord. In these areas she presents herself and matures because witnessing is also connected with these things.

Two men have taken a stand against the evaporation of the concept of the church. They must be considered here. Johannes Blauw demonstrates that the nature of the church consists in fellowship with Christ, and that κέρυγμα, διακονία, and λειτουργία (proclamation, service, and worship) must be viewed together and performed in close relation to each other.

How easily the mission loses the connection with the other vital expressions of the church! Admittedly one can say that

[37] ". . . The church is the congregation of saints in which the Gospel is rightly taught and the sacraments rightly administered. To the true unity of the church it is enough to agree concerning the doctrine of the Gospel and the administration of the sacraments. Nor is it necessary that human traditions, that is, rites or ceremonies instituted by men, should be everywhere alike."

[38] W. Elert, *Der christliche Glaube* (Berlin: Furche Verlag, 1955), p. 419.

> there is only one function of the church: the *missio* or the apostolate; but one always knows that this is not so and cannot be so. That all vital expressions of the church must be directed toward witnessing is quite another matter. . . . But with the same right one can say that everything in the church should be directed to the praise of God, to worship, hence *also* the mission.[39]

Moreover, it is mainly van Ruler who recognizes the weaknesses of the doctrine concerning the apostolate, is aware of its discrepancies in the proper understanding of the church, and seeks to study the whole matter anew.

> The nature of the apostolate of the church does not consist in this that it goes out into the world, there gives its witness, and occupies a place in the world, but it consists in this that it is used. She (the church) is an instrument.

Here the church is presented as a divinely ordained entity over against the apostolate. But the latter is further defined by him from the viewpoint of predestination: It (the apostolate) is not an attribute; that would be an ecclesiological contraction. It is more than a mandate, otherwise the church could lapse into activism. It is more than witness-bearing, otherwise the church would be subject to humanization.

"The apostolate is the nature of the church," she is God's tool.[40] However appealing these limitations are, they do not as yet hit the nail on the head. The nature of the church actually consists in her purpose. Jesus Christ as the Head of the church has made her His body, confers on her His fellowship, joins the members unto Himself, permeates her by Word and Sacrament to make her a church. He creates her, empowers her, brands her with all the marks of discipleship, and gives her an assignment. From all of these gifts bestowed

[39] J. Blauw, "Mission lebt von der Kirche," *Die Botschaft von Jesus Christus in einer nichtchristlichen Welt* (n. p., 1952), p. 16.

[40] van Ruler, p. 7.

87

by Him and from this life in Christ there arises the apostolate, which certainly has no other goal than to lead the church in service for the salvation of mankind.

> She has been chosen out of the world for that very purpose, that she render unto the world that ministry which the world most needs and which consists precisely in this that she give to the world the witness concerning Jesus Christ and call it to faith in Him. She would have forgotten her election and forfeited it if she had existed only for herself and neglected this ministry, if she did not actually transmit.[41]

Our objections are furthermore confirmed by another line of thought which is of great importance to the Dutch brethren as well as to Karl Barth, but which in Holland is thought of entirely in the light of election. It is the idea of the people of God. Here, too, we must take the time to study the Biblical evidence.

17. The New People of God

A mission without a clear concrete sending does not exist. Sending takes place not in some dynamic operation of the congregation, but in the concrete transfer of the ministry and in instruction. On the one hand, this is bestowed in the priesthood of all believers along with Baptism, but it becomes an actual sending in the world where messengers are called and sent out. The congregation would not be entitled to this if it were not, as already indicated, a member of the *missio Dei*. Through the *missio Dei* the same thing happens to the church as we already established earlier when dealing with God's role.

As God Himself in His *missio* confronts the world and yet through His sending establishes His relationship to the world, so He now gives to His church the same position which He holds. The church, of course, is always in danger of identifying itself with the world, being absorbed by it, or

[41] Barth, II, 2 (1942), p. 217.

establishing its solidarity with the people. The danger is especially great because of the following reasons: All religions think that fellowship of religion is fellowship of culture and people and, secondly, all countries endeavor to guarantee the unity of their people through unity of religion. The danger is always immanent in the church because, by sheer necessity, she becomes a fellowship into which a person is born.

The church can ward off this danger if, on the one hand, she realizes that through the *missio* she is placed completely on the side of God and, if on the other hand, she realizes that she is fully directed to the world. She is placed on the side of God because her members have through Christ Jesus been "loved out" of this world and placed together in the congregation of the new people of God. To this new people of God all the attributes apply just as the people of the Old Testament had them (1 Peter 2:9). Through these attributes she is distinguished from the world.

In her life and in her attitude the church is different from the world. She does not belong to herself or to the world, but to God. In her the life that flows from Christ is manifest. For that reason she is an epistle of Christ to the world, visible and legible to the world (2 Cor. 3:3). In the midst of the world of darkness she is the light; amid corruption she is the salt. But she is this not of *herself*, but of *God*. And she is this not for *herself*, but for the *world*. For that reason one can only speak of the nature of the congregation when one looks at her from God's standpoint and determines from God's side what the church is. Thus only through the *missio Dei* can the true nature of the church become evident.

This tells us that the congregation in the world must function primarily through her presence. The church is either a congregation for witness, ministry, and doxology, or she is no church of Jesus Christ.

89

She is the one who with her knowledge and experience of God's grace becomes proxy and stands surety for the remainder of the world which has not as yet become partaker of the testimonies of the Holy Ghost. Over against the world the church in her special role is placed into the service of reconciliation as a witness of the grace of God.[42] The gathering and renewing of the church are not an end in themselves, but promote the sending of the church into the world — the church which is the light of the world and the salt of the earth, not by the might of man but by the power of Christ through the world-shaking dynamic of the kingdom of God that came into the world, still comes, and will come.[43]

The entire congregation, through its life, through its word from person to person, through its contacts which the individual member has with his fellow beings, imparts the word and should be an attraction for all men.

For this reason it is clear that Christ has not given the church a distinct missionary office. He did give her an office which should lead to missionary service — namely, the ministry of the divine Word in its fullness. The missionary witness is included in this. Therefore everything that the church has been told concerning her pastoral office can be applied primarily to the missionary service of the church (2 Cor. 3-5). Accordingly, the pastoral office in the congregation in all its ramifications can have no other purpose than to lead the congregation to influence the world and to make her fit for missionary service. Everything which has been offered to the congregation for edification should serve that purpose. All other offices which this one office includes find therein their common orientation, their mutually subordinate position, and their highest destiny — that they serve the sending. Where this is clearly understood, the mission is no longer a problem

[42] K. Barth, IV, 1 (1953), p. 166.

[43] H. D. Wendland, *Die Kirche in der modernen Gesellschaft* (Hamburg: Furche-Verlag, 1956), p. 103.

but the fulfillment of every ministry which takes place in and for the congregation.

But when the pastoral office, because of dogmatic restriction serves only the welfare, administration, and self-support of the church, it is humanly limited in a self-centered way. When the office merely endeavors to edify the congregation and to achieve the salvation of individual members, it is questionable whether the goal of mission is attained because this does not provide the members with the chance to find joy in their faith through service and sacrifice. When the opportunity for obedience and service is missing, the living stream of the Word cannot flow. This is often the reason why the individual members themselves no longer treasure this Word. Thus the pastoral office unintentionally becomes a hindrance to mission work among the heathen instead of a missionary impulse. The incumbents of the office are then the ones that close the door to heaven. (Matt. 23:13)

The true shape of the congregation appears where it is clearly understood that the Word and the congregation are an indissoluble unity. They are so closely related to each other that what is said about the Word is readily applied to the congregation. The report of the conference in Whitby [44] clearly set this forth.[45] The Word of God and the church are often treated in Scripture as such a unity. This becomes clear already in the parables of Matt. 13 and Mark 4. It is pointedly expressed in the Book of Acts, where the growth of the Word is explicitly mentioned when the growth of the congregation is meant (Acts 6:7; 12:24; 19:20). This can only mean, on the one hand, that along with the congregation also the working power and the working area of the Word grows because the Holy Ghost receives increasingly more possibilities

[44] Cf. chapter IV, footnote 3.

[45] Freytag, *Der grosze Auftrag*, pp. 32 ff.

91

through the multitude of witnesses. On the other hand, this means that the office which has to proclaim the Word must always keep in mind the expansion of the church. The Word itself therefore takes on a shape of its own in the congregation and becomes in the congregation a life-giving and self-propagating Word.

18. Church and World

When the *missio Dei* becomes actualized in this way, the effective task of the congregation must be understood as the spreading of the Word in her relation to the world. In order to be able to spread the Word the congregation must always recognize in the world, in unbelieving fellowmen, its opposite number which it must confront with its life and faith. Where the church recognizes her "otherness" and preserves it, this attitude will follow spontaneously. The greatest weakness of Christianity today is that Christians no longer know that they are Christians. They have lost their power as salt.

> So long as this world stands, the concrete confrontation of church and non-church can no more be done away than the relationship of Israel to other nations, in spite of all fluctuations in that relationship. In this encounter between two peoples, God speaks to the world. He speaks to it in such a way that His Word creates the church in order that then, through the service of the church, that Word becomes the Word to the world.[46]

We are here facing the tensions of the true relationship between church and people, and church and world respectively — a problem which constantly confronted evangelical theology in Germany and one to which it capitulated in part. The new self-examination of the mission on this point had already taken place before the war. Since G. Warneck constantly sought a Christianization of people as the goal of the mission and identified a Christian people with the folk

[46] Barth, I, 2 (1938), p. 769.

church, a new self-examination was absolutely necessary. Hartenstein and Walter Freytag had, prior to the war, tried to find new approaches to the problem. The former strictly preserved in his theological writings a distinction between the church and people; the latter calls the congregation the point of breakthrough for the Holy Ghost in the world. Church and congregation have the duty to lead men to the obedience of faith. For both of them the ministry of the congregation is determined by the coming kingdom.

Hoekendijk's criticism above all began with this German concept of the nation and nationality promoted by various theologians and mission scholars and determined by Romanticism. In order to determine the proper place of the congregation in the world and over against the nation, the Dutch mission scholars made inquiries into the propaedeutic significance of the Old Testament people of God, for the nature of the church and its attitude over against the world.

Sad to say, a contribution not sufficiently recognized was given by Albrecht Oepke,[47] who even though he did not lay down guidelines for the mission on the basis of his insights nevertheless said something of decisive importance for the church. He showed how the idea of the people of God was a determining factor for the proper understanding of the New Testament church, showing that through this concept the early church had achieved proper understanding of itself.

Johannes Blauw [48] has given us the most thorough essay on this question, in which he investigated what the Holy Scriptures mean by the word "heathen." Since the heathen are the *vis-a-vis* of God's people, it was necessary to investigate just what the Scriptures mean by "God's people."

[47] *Das neue Gottesvolk* (Gütersloh: C. Bertelsmann, 1950).

[48] Johannes Blauw. *Goden en Mensen* (Groningen: J. Niemeijer, 1950).

The surprising thing is that the various investigators come to the same conclusions. Israel's election was a call to service. She was to impress the world so that, by the example of Israel, the rule of God would become evident to the nations. Thus the election of Israel already at this time had cosmic significance and eschatological direction. From this viewpoint through the self-understanding of the church as the new people of God, the church's attitude to nation and world results. She stands over against the world and therefore is sent to the world. Her ministry is therefore quantitatively unlimited and she must embrace all mankind. Admittedly, a qualitative limitation arises, for the church as the bearer of revelation must stand for the truth and must confront the world with the question of truth. Only if the church desires in all things to be God's people, and thereby also the church of Jesus Christ, will she be able to develop the strongest impact on the world.

Therefore her special stance becomes the presupposition for the universality of her ministry. From this it follows that the church may be only God's people among the nations.[49] These ideas were most strongly developed at the World Mission Conference in Willingen,[50] where participants came to the understanding of the mission here noted. They designated

[49] Ibid., pp. 63 ff.

[50] Here a "missions" conference first used the little boat afloat, symbol of the Ecumenical Movement. "It appears to be adrift on the open sea with no land in sight, utterly at the mercy of the wind, wave, and storm. What port is it making for? From which port did it set out crewless and forlorn? What haven will give it shelter? It appears to be abandoned: but it is right side up still, and plumb in its middle is the Cross braving the tides and currents, and obviously giving guidance to the little boat, not just rocking at its moorings but out on its voyage across the oceans of time." Cecil Northcott, *Christian World Mission* (London: Lutterworth Press, 1952), pp. 34 ff. (Tr.)

the church as the pilgrim people of God, which lives in tents and carries out His ministry until He comes.[51]

Through these insights the idea set forth above, that predestination and the apostolate are interrelated, is more thoroughly established, and, on the other hand, the danger of a purely dynamic understanding of the church is pointed out. In other words, when the church regards itself as the people of God, we must understand that she is *NOT* to be understood as an institution, or permanent residence and immobility, as being hemmed in by national boundaries, *BUT* the church must somehow take shape in order to be able to confront the world.

It is precisely when she carries on the apostolate that the church must take on a shape all her own. These thoughts, however, are crowded into the background by the fear that through regarding herself as an organization the church could concern herself so much with her own affairs that she might no longer witness to the world. The danger obviously is evident in every form of the church. No form of church organization guarantees that she will not put on the armor of organization again and again and thereby become sterile. Rather she should, through her service in the world, always allow herself to be crowded into the ghetto. For when this takes place through the pressure of the world, then the church clearly shows that it is influencing the world.

If because of these dangers one would eliminate the idea of the church, then one would also lose the idea of the apostolate. A genuine apostolate is possible only where the church is a fully visible reality which expresses itself in confession. Through this the catholicity of the church is not hampered; instead, the church achieves her global diversity, which also is implicit in her ethnic emphasis. The apostolate accordingly

[51] Hartenstein, as quoted in W. Freytag, *Mission zwischen Gestern und Morgen* (Stuttgart: Evangelischer Missionsverlag, 1952), pp. 53 ff.

does not lead to something shoreless; it does not blur the boundaries. When we look at things from the viewpoint of the nature of the church, the apostolate itself results in the distinct characteristics of the individual churches.

It is significant that in the framework of the special position of the church there is no mention of the meaning of the sacraments. However, the true church always maintains her place in the world in that she meets for her divine services, permits herself to be drawn into fellowship with her Lord in the Sacrament, and works on the world with power received through the Word and Sacrament. She can only hand on that life which she allows to be given to her. Of course, she must pass it on if she wishes to keep it, otherwise it will die. The attitude of the church to the world, therefore, is shown not merely in the fact that God entrusted her with the treasure of the Word and Sacrament but in order that through these she should preach reconciliation to the world. This ministry, which makes her a member of the *missio Dei,* gives the church the attitude which she needs to reach her missionary goal.

THE MISSIONARY GOAL

MUCH THAT COULD BE SAID under this heading has already been said and indicated, for one cannot speak of the motivation for missions without at the same time having its goal in view, the final outcome which supplies the motivation. Thus we will endeavor to restrict ourselves to what has not as yet been said, especially the formation of the church.

1. The Conversion of the Nations

The church is placed into the world and sent by her Lord into the world. This is her environment; with respect to it she has an assignment. She is to proclaim to the lost world, the non-Christians, the message of redemption and through the reception of the message on the part of the hearers to gather a congregation of the redeemed, God's people on earth.

Who are these non-Christians, the heathen? The missionary command directs the church with her message to πάντα τὰ ἔθνη, to all nations. This term has long posed several great questions for the mission. In German missiology especially it becomes a central concept. G. Warneck has declared it to be the purpose of the mission in opposition to Pietism's idea of gathering only such as would allow themselves to be converted. According to Warneck individuals were not to be gained, rather the nations. His followers included his students Richter, Frick, Knak, and also the missionaries Gutmann and Keysser. All of them understood "nations" to mean not a casual number of people of a special group, one language, or a certain state, but they viewed the nations as organic entities and societies, characterized by nationality and religion, in their ordered relationship, thus organisms with a solid sociological structure and ethnic identity.

In this way, ethnic individualities took the place of the individuals in Pietism. Each nation, in its specific character-istics, is therefore to be christianized and these characteristics are to be placed into the service of the Gospel so that the nation can be transferred into the church. The ongoing process of an individual conversion was not meant, which, if correctly applied, could also gradually lead to the gaining of all the nation's members; rather, the conversion and christianization of the communities as such.

The men mentioned above were sober-minded enough to know that the goal could only be reached by stages and only to a certain degree. Each of the men, primarily the two mis-sionaries, tried to use methods which recommended them-selves on the basis of the nationality with which they were dealing. None of the men wanted to eliminate the funda-mental missionary work of proclamation; none thought of bypassing individual decision. That must be kept in mind because it is so easily overlooked in the critique.

Precisely because they formulated the missionary goal in the way they did, the missionaries were compelled to take the other side very seriously and to leave room for an independent decision for the Gospel. They also knew that a man can never be won as an isolated being. He is always somehow influenced in his decisions by his fellowmen, regardless of whether he be-longs to an anonymous multitude or an organic community. Consequently the community must be permeated by the mes-sage if the individual is to be gained.

The conversion of the nations provided a great and re-warding goal which lifted missionary work out of its narrow confines and gave it a great pedagogical task. This task consisted in leading the nations toward Christian objectives, meanwhile exercising the most circumspect regard for their own national selfhood so that from the synthesis of Gospel and nationality a distinctive and self-sustaining culture might arise. Experience seemed to justify the advocates of this goal, for where it was attempted, vital churches, deeply rooted in the people, came into being. The christianizing of the nations as the goal of mission work was largely taken over by the Continental missions, even though pursued with various modifications. Especially German thinking on missions was influenced by what Hoekendijk terms "ethnic fervor."

The increasingly vigorous expansion of western civilization with its demoralizing effects on the nations, and the emphasis on a standard Christianity by the Anglo-Saxon missions rallied German missiologists to defend ever more stoutly a Christianity synthesized with nationhood. The dangers of placing nationality above the Gospel or of reading more into the Gospel than was said about nationality were not always seen and considered. Only with Hartenstein and Freytag was the previously mentioned new concept introduced which sharply distinguished the congregation from its natural environment.

During the last war the danger of this mission theory was powerfully illustrated by the excesses of nationalism. Therefore this theory came under severe criticism led by Hoekendijk.[1] His book ought to call the German mission to its senses. German Protestant theology owes him an answer. He has supplied sufficient challenges from the fields of church history, exegesis, systematics, and the science of missions. But sad to say, the book, with its profound and fundamental arguments has been ignored until now. Either German theology has lived such an introverted life that it pays no atten-

[1] J. C. Hoekendijk, *Kerk en Volk in de duitse Zendingswetenschap* (Utrecht: Proefschrift, 1948).

tion to such publications or it regards itself superior to what an expert on missions has to say.

2. *The Concept* τὰ ἔϑνη

In the critique of Hoekendijk a good deal is justified, primarily the rebuke (pp. 229 f.) that German mission theology has translated too naively the concept of τὰ ἔϑνη with "nations" and by this translation has even applied the meaning of the Romantic concept of "nation" in which, through Pietistic influence, the individual characteristics of every nation were still stressed. On the other hand, it appears to us a bit hasty for Hoekendijk to make Luther and Lutheranism responsible for this understanding of the concept, even though Hoekendijk can appeal to two important research scholars.

Here Johannes Dürr [2] is fairer concerning Warneck and the German theology of missions when he attempts to prove that Gustav Warneck — although himself a Biblicist and friend of the Pietists — sought to set forth, in contrast to the Pietistic mission goal of gaining the individual soul and gathering it into Christian communities, the winning of nations, hence all men, and the establishment of a national church. He also justified this goal not only with Scripture passages, but also with historical and missionary experience.

Further, it must likewise be regarded as unfair when Hoekendijk believes he has to establish that Warneck and his students consequently did not regard the church as a historical factor for salvation, but rather permitted it to be molded by the people so that the church would be understood more or less as a cultural factor. In the thinking of Warneck and his pupils the eschatological boundary was perhaps not set

[2] Johannes Dürr, *Sendende und werdende Kirche in der Missionstheologie G. Warneck's* (Basel: Basler Missionsbuchhandlung, 1947), pp. 146 ff. Dürr, at present professor at Bern, was formerly missionary to Moslems in Indonesia.

forth with the precision or clarity with which we can do it now, since Karl Barth and Oscar Cullmann. However, in view of the fact that Warneck, in spite of his worldwide conception of missions, always understood the actual congregation in the Pietistic sense as the group of believers, Hoekendijk could have said that Warneck also realized the confrontation of church and nation. Thus on these points Hoekendijk goes too far.

As much as we acknowledge valid points in Hoekendijk's critique, we must now, on the other hand, carefully test to what extent he is correct. In the process we must first administer to him a rebuke much like the one we direct against the German mission scholars. If these German scholars translate τὰ ἔθνη too naively with "nations," Hoekendijk somewhat too easily and apodictically renders it "humanity" or πάντα τὰ ἔθνη as "all men" without their nationalistic involvement, and therefore understands πάντα τὰ ἔθνη as referring to "people outside of the nation of Israel," in other words, in terms of salvation history.

Without allowing ourselves here to enter upon a detailed study of the term — we refer the interested reader to the *Theologisches Woerterbuch zum Neuen Testament* [3] — we must first of all raise the question: Even if ἔθνη is to be understood from the standpoint of salvation history, is it possible to think of men without their national characteristics? Also from the viewpoint of salvation history man is still seen in his natural environment. ἔθνος is also used in Scripture for an association of people and can also be applied to Israel. When ἔθνη is connected with πάντα, it means nations in the collective as well as in their variety (Matt. 24:9; 24:14; 25:32; 28:19; Mark 11:17; 13:10; Luke 21:24; 24:47; Rom. 11:25; Gal.

[3] K. L. Schmidt, ἔθνος, *Theologisches Wörterbuch zum Neuen Testament,* ed. Gerhard Kittel (Stuttgart: W. Kohlhammer Verlag, 1933) II, 366—369.

3:8). In other passages the term is used exclusively in connection with salvation history, namely, in contrast to the people of Israel (Matt. 6:7; Luke 12:30; Matt. 10:5; 20:19; Acts 14:16). Matthew 28:19, on which Warneck bases his mission goal, is not included here.

The variety within the nations also includes the heathen religion. However, this does not prove that ἔθνη can simply be translated as "heathen" or "men," as little as πάντα τὰ ἔθνη is the equivalent for πᾶσα κτίσις or ἅπας κόσμος, as Hoekendijk assumes. To be sure, the question arises whether German missiology was correct, since ἔθνη already in the Old Testament is a very elusive term which no longer transmits the awareness that the plural denotes the majority of the nations in their uniqueness. Thus the term ἔθνη means the people outside of Israel without regard for their sociological character.

Also at the time of the New Testament the term was thus understood in the Greek world. The Romans used it to designate the non-Romans, as well as strangers and barbarians. Thus the term could also express the cultural contrast. Therefore we can say that ἔθνη is a term which includes men and nations outside of God's congregation or outside of the dominant culture. We must leave it an open question whether they are to be viewed against their sociologically and nationalistically determined background. Warneck's missionary goal that the nations are to be christianized, can therefore not be established from the missionary command. Also the idea that ethnic ordinances ought to be maintained cannot be established from the mere concept ἔθνη.

3. The Missionary Goal

We must first of all describe this as the winning of all men and gathering them into the church of Christ. No one stands outside the kingdom of God. The Gospel is intended for all men. The nations as ἔθνη form a unity over against the congregation of God because they are lost in sin. The lost condition which all men have in common ties them together, as they are also united in the promise that all men are to be saved. They all should come to the knowledge of the truth (2 Tim. 2:4). The truth was already present in Israel. It has received the revelation. Hence Israel is not included in the sense of salvation history among the ἔθνη, which would be the case if Israel were spoken of only as a nation. Revelation determines this decisive contrast. (1 Thess. 4:5, cf. Jer. 10:25)

The "all" in the mission command is very clearly underlined by Matt. 24:14. No one among the heathen is excluded. The message is to be proclaimed in the entire οἰκουμένη, which is the living space of the nations and thus the sphere of the church's proclamation. Thus the οἰκουμένη and the κόσμος become correlates of the βασιλεία and the opposite number to the *missio Dei* and apostolate. Therefore the goal of the mission is the proclamation of the message to all mankind and gathering them into the church.

However, Scripture does not say that this goal will be reached. It lies in the nature of the revelation and thereby in the nature of God that every person will be addressed. The possibility of believing and of redemption is given to man. However, Scripture is realistic enough not to leave us unaware that only a portion of mankind will accept the message. Since one cannot ascertain who is in this portion, the church has the responsibility for all of humanity.

4. The Peculiarities of Nations

Upon arriving at this clarification, we may again raise the question concerning the meaning of the term "nation" as an organized association within the framework of the missionary goal. We cannot avoid the term since man, viewed from the point of salvation history, is still the creature of God and the object of His love even though he does not belong

103

to the congregation. To begin with, a weighty question arises in Matt. 28:19. If one understands ἔθνη purely from the viewpoint of salvation history, is the mission command still intended for Israel? Is mission to the Jews still justified? We know that the revelation of God in Jesus Christ was intended primarily for Israel. Then what becomes of apostate Israel when only the heathen are meant by the term ἔθνη?

If one understands ἔθνη as humanity in its national varieties, then no doubt remains that "the nations" before God are a unity in their lost sinful condition. Humanity must be saved precisely in its varieties. Dare we simply place the differences as they exist in language and in sociological and social customs on the same level as the heathen religions, and thereby label them as the expression of apostasy and rebellion? Cannot many of these customs be thought of apart from the respective religions? Are they not, under the circumstances, a reflection of man's dependence upon God? Were not the linguistic differences, for example, at the outpouring of the Holy Ghost, taken very seriously? Isn't it true according to Scripture that man sins precisely in customs which he has unconsciously adopted and thereby transgresses against God? In any case, it is striking that according to Romans 1 and 2 the heathen are responsible before God in the same degree as the Jews, and of course as heathen! They know about the relationship of the sexes and marriage, about the parent-child relationship, and about the sanctity of human life.

When we study the so-called catalogs of vices it strikes us that the trespasses of the heathen against God are at the same time trespasses against their own regulations. Thus man sins within the ordinances which God has given to him. They are, to be sure, commandments which are also laid down in God's revelation. Johannes Blauw asserts that the Bible always speaks of the heathen as it speaks of natural man. The latter sins without revelation and, in fact, in such a way that he transgresses against his own laws. But as little as the revelation is set aside because man does not know it, so little are the ordinances set aside because the conscience is unreliable. It is self-evident that one cannot write a theology of ordinances, as has repeatedly been done; the base is too narrow.[4]

To this extent Hoekendijk is right when he takes this kind of theology to task. God has in His revelation set up other ordinances which are to come into force through His congregation. However, He has also sanctified existing ordinances and placed them under His command. Therefore the congregation alone can decide — and that only on the basis of Scripture — what concerns of nationality can be recognized as valid from time to time under the application of the Gospel.

God has also given to the congregation the commandment of love and thereby all ordinances in the human realm have taken on an entirely new meaning. A certain ethnic determination is also connected with the term ἔθνη which is not set aside through the law of love. Where indeed should love reveal itself as love if not especially in the obligations which determine the life of men together? Thus we must be clear that a number of ordinances which we regard as self-evidently Christian are not rooted in the Sacred Scriptures but have their origin in the modern image of man and therefore often run counter to Biblical thought without our feeling we have the right to oppose them.

However, from the standpoint of Scripture, the same thing

[4] The idea can best be explained by quoting a portion of the Willingen I. M. C. Conference statement: "We summon all Christians to come forth from the securities which are no more secure and from the boundaries of accepted duty too narrow for the Lord of the earth, and to go forth with fresh assurance to the task of bringing all things into captivity to Him, and of preparing the whole world for the day of His coming." Cecil Northcott, *Christian World Mission* (London: Lutterworth Press, 1952), p. 34. "Cancelling the bond of ordinances that held us, He set it aside, nailing it to His cross" (Col. 2:14). (Tr.)

holds true whether one adopts old ordinances or introduces those that have come into being in a different human society. Also these latter offer the congregation no guarantee of a genuine confrontation. Ordinances emphasize at best the alien character of the church. Every ordinance is basically a danger to the church if it is not fostered by men who through regeneration know that Jesus makes all things new.

5. The Christians Among the Heathen

In two New Testament passages Christians are called heathen, ἔθνη (Rom. 11:3; Eph. 3:1). That certainly does not mean that these Christians stand outside of the revelation of God, as do the other ἔθνη, and that they have no claim to this revelation. All that can be gathered from this is that, in contrast to Jewish Christians, they have other patterns of living and at the same time, through the grace of God, they are counted among God's people. With considerable passion Paul wages his attack against the Judaizing of the Gentile Christian congregations. They would have laid a yoke upon themselves by adopting Jewish patterns of living. Paul would not have been so vehement had he believed that one could become a Christian only by way of Judaism. It is precisely this that he negated.

The wonderful thing about the Gospel is that under the Word of God man may become fully that which he is by birth. Paul also permitted the social relations as adapted to the people to remain in the congregations. He did not see the hallmark of Christianization in the transmission of new social patterns. Rather, he was sure the new life created by the Gospel would find for itself a place in these ordinances and would transcend them. When Hoekendijk concludes that one cannot appeal with "ethnic fervor" to the Old Testament, where national and religious fellowship in Israel are identical, he is right. If one does this, one overlooks the fact that Israel is in a class by itself where in an extraordinary way that which is understood by the word "nation" has been formed by God.

Nationality does not determine religion, but religion determines nationality. Religion is formed by revelation. Besides, a distinction must be made between God's covenant with the tribes and the political organization of Israel, which is something different. Moreover, the appearance of the prophets proves that the national fellowship and the congregation of God were not identical. We can acknowledge all this and yet must ask: Did not also the ordinances of the heathen nations have a right to be placed under the judgment of God, and can they not also, under the judgment of God, be completely determined by God? Certainly we do not have the political task to regulate the nation, but we do have the task to call the nations to repentance so that their relationship with God may be regulated. Can the result be anything else than that the social patterns of the nations are made new by the Gospel?

Hoekendijk would agree with us in all of these questions, but he would object that the yardstick for this change could in no case be based on the nations. (Neither do we desire this.) Hoekendijk would rather say that the congregation could attain its special position only if it bases itself entirely on the Gospel. Thus it would always wear the features of its environment because the Gospel always takes shape in the environment, but the ordinances are not indicated for it in the nation. Hoekendijk calls this process ecology. With this he offers the solution to the problem. Thus he says that every nation presents a unique environment for the Gospel and for the congregation. The congregation will adjust itself to the environment just as an animal or plant. The environment exerts a certain influence but, nevertheless, it does not transform. Just so with the Christian congregation. It will always

107

wear a local costume but it will nevertheless remain faithful to itself and not sell out to the nation.[5]

6. The Pedagogical Boundary

When Warneck recommended national education through missions, and thereby sought a gradual christianizing of the ordinances, he no doubt wanted to bring these ordinances under the judgment of God; but the presupposition was that for the time being they could remain. He was aware of the dangers. It is unusual that on the basis of experience he did not believe in some kind of sharp break. Thereby he limited his Biblical insights. Thus a certain two-track attitude is evident in Warneck which, theologically viewed is a weakness in his teaching on missions. When such men as Knak — in his theoretical insights — and Gutmann, as well as Keysser, in their congregational practice, whether consciously or unconsciously, ultimately seek a synthesis of sacred and profane history, there certainly is the danger of stripping sacred history of its ontological character and of setting up a kind of theocracy in profane history. But this applies not only to these men.

There are many young churches in the world concerning which one asks himself whether it is a question of a Christianized nation or a nationalized Christianity. But on the other hand, these methods offered great opportunities to bring all branches of life under the Word of God and thus permeate

[5] One could pursue this question further by looking at the Batak Protestant Christian Church, the largest Lutheran Church outside the Western world. It is a member of the Lutheran World Federation but has never adopted the 16th-century Lutheran confessions. Rather than adopt the Augsburg Confession, the Bataks have drawn up their own, the first Asian church so far to do this. *The Confession of Faith of the Huria Kristen Batak Protestant* was adopted by the Great Synod in the November 1951 meeting at Sipholon-Tarutung. Vilmos Vajta and Hans Weissgerber, eds., *The Church and the Confessions* (Philadelphia: Fortress, 1963), pp. 139—147. (Tr.)

all of life. Hoekendijk has recognized the weaknesses, but desires to hold fast to the benefits through ecology. Viewed as a whole, the question forces itself upon us whether Hoekendijk, in his concern to preserve the special position of the congregation, has fallen into a Pietistic limitation which is not removed by his recommendation of the "comprehensive approach."

The questions concerning nation and nationality, the indigenous character of the church, are of eminent importance today for the young churches which must suffer under nationalism and thereby under the reproach of being alien. Their striving for independence is certainly not only a reaction against church expansion and colonization, but a struggle for their own development in their environment. Surely this whole matter merits ongoing discussion.

This concern was pressed anew through the essays of MacGavran [6] and Spencer Trimingham,[7] who demonstrated [8] that the church and mission can have success in expansion only if they offer their message through natural channels such as kinship and friendship, where they can be passed on from one to the other. Thus no social break is created. The convert has connection with his family and kin. The congregation from its inception would become a social force to

[6] Dr. Donald A. MacGavran, educated in the United States, served as a missionary in India since 1923, and is at present head of the Institute for Church Growth at Eugene, Oreg. He is recognized as a prominent spokesman for the missionary strategy of winning people for Christ by families and groups rather than as individuals. Cf. MacGavran, *The Bridges of God* (New York: The Friendship Press, 1955). (Tr.)

[7] The Rev. J. Spencer Trimingham, at present serving as lecturer in Arabic at Glasgow University, has been a missionary in the Sudan and Egypt. He is most widely known for his study of Islam. Cf. *The Christian Church and Islam in West Africa* (London: SCM Press, 1955). (Tr.)

[8] MacGavran, op. cit., Trimingham, op. cit.

supply security and transform society. For the young churches one of the most burning questions today is, whether they can put Christian principles to work with decisive effect in building up the nation. Whether that is possible will depend to a large extent on how deeply the church has come to grips with the problems of its own distinctive and inherited culture.

7. Missions and Civilization

Did Hoekendijk go too far in his critique? Is he affected too much by the image of modern man? In any case he demonstrates that, due to the tremendous influence of a universal civilization, nationalistic characteristics no longer have a future today. People do not want to keep on dragging their own social forms along anymore, but seek inclusion in the "great society," the family of mankind created by civilization. At the time of the publication (1949) of his book, Hoekendijk was generally right. In the meantime nationalism has changed the nations.[9] It seems that the crisis has been passed and the ethnic characteristics are again very strongly emphasized. Thereby the previous questions once more become decisive issues for every young church and every mission.

Hoekendijk recommends the "comprehensive approach" in this situation. Accordingly all areas of man's life are to be permeated with Christian thoughts so that men learn how one can be and act the Christian in all things. He has basically the same goal as the strategy of nationalism, namely, to permit nothing to remain extraneous to God.[10] The main question is just what one understands by "Christian." Only in a few cases does the Bible give concrete directions. The result is that the "comprehensive approach" passes on as Chris-

[9] Cf. Rajah B. Manikam, *Christianity and the Asian Revolution* (New York: The Friendship Press, 1954), pp. 118 ff. (Tr.)

[10] E. Jansen Schoonhoven, "Wort und Tat im Zeugendienst," *Mission — Heute* (1954).

110

tian that which we consider Christian, viz. our civilization. But do we have a right to transmit this? Is it Christian because it was developed through centuries of history together with Christendom? Does not actually the same thing happen here which the other methods based on nationalism want to accomplish? I fear that the problems arising here are worse than those in connection with the folk or national approach.

The problem in this approach is not the existing, indigenous factors, but the inability of the missionary to recognize their value and to come to terms with these factors through the congregation.[11] As long as the missionary with his alleged Christian way of life stands above the people he will hardly consider the "raw" material on hand useful and capable of further development. He will, accordingly, repudiate it. But that way no genuine confrontation at all takes place! This confrontation then must be called, not "Gospel vis-a-vis nationalism," but "civilization vis-a-vis nationalism," and the latter is worse than that attempted by a mission program directed to the people as a whole.

Up to the present day very few missionaries have understood what genuine contact and debate is. This can never proceed in any other way than the way in which God through Jesus Christ has Himself made contact. He came as a man to a very definite people and lived under the same conditions as those under which this nation had to live. Thus He shared in bearing the misery of the nation and, under the same conditions in which the people had to prove their faith in God, showed His fellowmen how one could, in all conditions of life, become and remain a child of God. He criticized many in-

[11] Cf. Vicedom's most recent word on the subject in "Der innere Wandel der Religionen als Frage an unsere Verkündigung," *Theologische Literaturzeitung*, LXXXVII (January 1962), pp. 15 ff. Here Vicedom makes the two-pronged thrust of first *knowing* the essentials of the religion one confronts and then *making a connection* between Christianity and the native religion and culture. (Tr.)

terpretations of the ordinances of His people. He debated with the leaders of the nation. Ever and again, He confronted the congregation of God, with Jewish conceptions of the Kingdom; but in all He remained a fellowman. Where the missionary succeeds in becoming that, many questions which theoretically are very weighty solve themselves.

We should not emphasize the social regulations of a nation to such an extent that they oppose the ordinances of love in the church. We also should not present them as the point of departure for the church. Neither dare we despise or downgrade them. We can only ask ourselves what God's Word says concerning this and how these ordinances can be formulated on that basis. We must also realize that every nationally-determined peculiarity of the church is an earthly dress; the relationship to nationality will only be right where one knows that this dress also is temporary.

This dress will be cast aside by the congregation more and more when it lives towards the Lord and permits itself to be molded by the new life determined through the Holy Ghost. The church must realize in any case that she dare not stress these peculiarities, for the church of Christ is composed of members from all nations and their unifying bond, their communal relationship, is the law of Christ under which she lives.

> National citizenship is not a preliminary stage for the reception of the Gospel. Nor is the effectual working of the Gospel the unfolding of national individuality . . . the characteristic thing is rather the intention of the Christian message which is universal and above nations and races.[12]

8. Step-by-Step Development

The Gospel of the Kingdom should be proclaimed to all men. All men should hear the message of salvation through

[12] Walter Künneth, *Politik zwischen Dämon und Gott* (Berlin: Lutherisches Verlagshaus, 1954), p. 194.

Jesus Christ. Thereby the immediate action of the messenger is indicated and the immediate goal of missions outlined. Gustav Warneck bases this proclamation on the missionary command and in the phrase μαϑητεύειν πάντα τὰ ἔϑνη places the emphasis on the μαϑητεύειν. He understood this as a great pedagogical direction; the hearer must be trained as a pupil to be a disciple.

Thus it was naturally up to the teacher to decide when the learner was to receive the diploma signifying maturity. Therefore Warneck does not understand the disciple relationship as a direct one, as we have described it. He knows that genuine disciples of Jesus would issue from mission work only in rare cases because many men would become Christians from secondary motives, would often remain stalled at the beginning of their disciple relationship and would sometimes defect again. Thus the desire to become a Christian would be sufficient. This desire should be acknowledged. Then every one with that expressed desire could grow and be trained into the disciple relationship. Whether this is to take place through the congregation or is brought about as the convert is sustained by the Christian ordinances of his nation remains quite immaterial.

Warneck, in good Catholic fashion, is here thinking entirely from the standpoint of practice. He is concerned not so much with evangelizing and therefore with conversion, but with Christianization, the national church. For those who have been won he would like to provide immediately a sphere of life influenced by a Christian atmosphere. To be sure, he uses the concepts such as to save, to convert, to become a believer, and to cling to the Lord. However, strange to say, he doubts that heathen Christians can at once have the full experience of faith. Warneck's reticence is all the more difficult to understand, since the heathen, previously untouched by the Word, certainly are confronted with the Gospel. This

113

produces a direct, first-hand experience, something much harder for the second generation to achieve.

Behind this stands the concept of the national church according to which one must be drawn into Christendom — the idea that the heathen Christian has as yet no tradition and thus could not be a Christian in the full sense of the word. Warneck is here thinking in a wholly pedagogical way. He views the Christianization of a nation in such a way that, to begin with, individuals are converted and these transmit the Word and their experience to others.

In this way the entire nation is gradually encompassed. It results in a development of tradition. That obviously requires a long time, generations under certain circumstances. Warneck has also here remained a Pietist, even though he advocates the national church. He still cannot conceive of the inclusion of a tribe or a nation called in its entirety under the Gospel so that the congregation of the baptized in its midst takes the lead and thereby determines the life of the nation.

9. The Evangelistic Method

According to Hoekendijk the church has the duty to witness to the Kingdom, to erect the signs of the Kingdom, and to preach the Gospel. Of course he is aware of the immediate goal of establishing a congregation, but does not mention this. He leaves it an open question whether and how the sermon becomes effective. This may be linked with predestination, according to which God on the basis of election decrees who comes to faith through the preaching of the Kingdom. Nevertheless, it is possible that Hoekendijk espouses the evangelistic method of missions according to which, on the basis of Matt. 24:14, it is enough when nations are brought under the witness. The formation of the message is not a goal worth striving after, but one leaves to the working of the Word whatever happens on the basis of the sermon. At the same time one is naturally grateful for every convert.

Through this method of proclaiming the Gospel to the heathen as quickly as possible as well as through Bible distribution the Word was transmitted to the heathen without their realizing that it calls for immediate decisions. The Word of God is turned over to the heathen without anyone watching over its correct interpretation and application or guarding it against abuse. In this way the evangelistic method prepared the way for syncretism. It is quite true that the Word of God itself works and that the Holy Ghost through the Word speaks to the heathen. However, one wonders whether a magical conception of the Word is championed here, which can in no way be justified from Scripture. The scanty results from this evangelistic method, however, prove that the Word of God unfolds no magical power.

When people come to faith in this manner, it always takes place through their contact with witnesses. It is an experience in Scripture, as well as of the mission, that the Holy Ghost always works through witnesses. The proclaimed Word which becomes evident in the hearer's life and which at the same time can be felt in the personality of the proclaimer has made an impression on the hearer. Seeing the example must always accompany the hearing. Without witnesses therefore, no one comes to Christ in the full sense of the word. Therefore Christianity always expands most energetically where the working of the Gospel becomes evident in a congregation or in a life.

It thus becomes clear just how important it is that by means of the sending the message becomes reality. Hence the message is also a part of human activity and competence in which, self-evidently, the working of the Spirit in the messenger is not called into question. The messenger himself, however, must also be obedient to the message and permit himself to be influenced by it. Certainly no human being can make anyone a believer, but nevertheless, very much depends on the conduct of the messenger. When Paul says in 1 Cor. 9:19 ff. that he had become a servant in order to gain some, or when he declares in Rom. 1:5 that he had received his office in order to bring about obedience of faith among the nations, he is saying to us at the same time, that the missionary must have a very concrete goal and that, of necessity, he will through his own conduct strive to remain faithful to this goal.

Accordingly one must exercise caution with the basically sound statement: "God must do everything." This is beyond question. But, always, God does His work only to the extent that His messenger has become an instrument. It is always decisive whether the messenger subordinates himself to God's doing. It is an open question as to how far the hearers accept the message and how this demonstrates itself in their lives. From the descriptions of the life of the church in the letters of the apostle, from his exhortations, and from his comparisons of the church with the heathen we can, in any case, conclude that also the churches of the New Testament were far from complete perfection, and yet Paul speaks of them in a laudatory way.

10. Becoming a Believer

If a contradiction arises here we must ask whether we correctly understand the process of becoming a believer. Do we not operate too much with theories and with the image of our own perfection or with our own understanding of faith and of Christianity, and thereby make ourselves the norm for the heathen Christians? To begin with, conversion and faith consist among all heathen Christians in the fact that they no longer do certain things because they have submitted themselves to God. But these things never include the entire life and thought. However, the fact remains that Christ has become their Lord and that they also want Him for their Savior. Therefore on very definite points where insights have been given to them they have become obedient and believing. Here the Word has compelled them to make a decision. As a result, a conversion has taken place which, however, in other points, must still become visible — a conversion which can continue to the degree that the hearer is guided by the Word.

It is a different story in the case of faith itself. In conversion faith is bestowed as confidence in God. Confidence in Him, dependence on Him, joy over the forgiveness of sins and certainty of redemption can also be present without a man's recognizing everything in his life that may contradict God. Through this step by step progress of the new life, which is always based on faith and which is given through the operation of the Holy Ghost, the man becomes more and more transfigured into the image of Christ.

To be sure, this faith can be shaken; it can be led into doubt. It undergoes changes. This is not to say that now the new life must also fluctuate. Man can cling to his insights. His life can be reshaped. According to Scripture there is a small faith and a large faith. There is a weak and a strong faith. But we don't hear that the weak faith may not be faith and that this faith could not be deepened. A great deal of our church practice is carried out to achieve this deepening. In all these forms of faith God is reality according to the measure of faith. Nevertheless, that does not alter the fact that also the person with a small or weak faith is a believer. Consequently, in our judgments concerning conversion and faith we ought to be very cautious. They are not such a simple process that one could pass judgment on them.

Also what he believes is certainly not left to the option of man. In all these forms of faith a relationship to Christ and therewith to God is present! A man who is far from God has no faith. The believer can always let himself be led farther by God from obedience to obedience.

Along with this obedience faith also grows. He can let himself be saturated by Jesus and become active in love. He can in faith let the measure of the Spirit be given to himself, and trusting in God he can lead a new life. However, where there is no faith, there is nothing. Faith is always the "Yes" to God's gracious working and thereby everything is included in God. How much more joy we would derive from the life of the converted heathen if we had the right understanding of faith.

11. The Means of the Mission

In order to lead men to faith, the messengers must fulfill their commission and thereby take up the battle against the other kingdom. The missionary command mentions the Word as the only means of the mission (Matt. 10:7; Luke 9:1 f.; Rom. 10:17). The proclamation is defined more exactly in 2 Cor. 5:19 as the preaching of reconciliation or paraphrased, "to testify to the Gospel of the grace of God" (Acts 20:24). The apostles did not proclaim this preaching as a system of doctrine, as a weltanschauung accommodated to human wisdom, but they always testified to the saving work of God with men.

Among the Jews they always began with the dealings of God with Israel; among the Gentiles they began with the creation and with the good things God had done for them. The resurrection is at the center of the preaching. He for whom God has not become reality may harbor within himself ever so much longing for salvation, yet he will never be able to grasp the fact that he cannot save himself. He who knows nothing of the Creator will decline God's claim. He who does not have the faintest inkling that there is a resurrection and a judgment will never understand his sins as a transgression

118

against God, nor will he regard himself responsible, and therefore he will also reject Jesus Christ as the Savior.

In Corinth, too, the resurrection was at the center of the preaching. If Paul, however, knew nothing save the cross, then it was for this reason: because the men of Corinth, influenced by Greek philosophy, believed they could be saved by human wisdom. He could preach no other salvation than the one that is given in the resurrection.

> Accordingly faith in the resurrection of Christ is an important part of the faith, not only in Christ, but in God. The death of Christ, alone, is the crisis of faith because it could have caused confusion about Christ or God. His resurrection overcomes the crisis, because in it the Father identifies Himself with the Son — as we would say when we use human analogies.[13]

Only through the proclamation of the entire work of Jesus Christ do men become fellowmen of Jesus Christ and participate in His history. Thus faith is not an opinion, a conviction gained by logical conclusions, but the certainty of the salvation history. This is what the apostles had to proclaim. We also can do this only in so far as salvation history has become our history through Christ, the history of God's working with us.

However, therewith only one side of the mission mandate and the means for its execution have been set forth. The kerygma must always be used in such a way that men hear it. They cannot of themselves come into the Kingdom, but they must be called in. They cannot become disciples if they do not listen to the call to follow. Thus the message must be presented in such a way that it will be heard and understood. The proclamation of the facts of salvation always refers the hearers to God and compels them to let their relationship to

[13] Werner Elert, *Der christliche Glaube* (Berlin: Furche Verlag, 1955), p. 302.

God be regulated by Him. God does this as He bestows upon believers the forgiveness of sins, justification, regeneration, in short, a new life, in which He preserves them through sanctification.

Where God's revelation strikes the hearers, something new always arises, i. e. a share in eternal life which consists of faith in Christ (John 17:3). Thereby the immediate goal of the proclamation is attained. Man is saved, snatched from the other kingdom; he has received a new existence. Even if we believe that this hearing is wrought by the Holy Ghost, yet what has been said of God's own activity is valid here. The hearing also comes through the witness. The hearing is at the same time understanding. When the preacher proclaims the Word in such a way that men cannot understand it, it remains an empty sound. If it is not brought to men in their language, they cannot grasp it. If the language is alien to them, it does not become God's own Word for men. The hearer must painstakingly seek to puzzle out the meaning.

But God wants to speak to man, and thus it is absolutely necessary that the language of the hearers is spoken by the messengers. The story of Lystra is a pertinent example of what takes place when one gives an opportunity to the hearers to misinterpret the message through the foreign language. God wants to draw so near to men in His proclamation that their entire person will be caught by it. Consequently the messenger must take pains to recast his sermon in foreign thought forms, to carry on an interior debate with the heathen environment so that he can proclaim the message of joy.

12. Mission and Miracle

The sending commission of the apostles has still a second aspect: "Heal the sick; raise the dead; cleanse the lepers; drive out evil spirits!" (Matt. 10:7, cf. Luke 9:1 f.; 10:9; in addition, the second Marcan ending). Here we face a very difficult question, which is again keenly felt just in our day. As we know, the apostles took this mandate seriously, for it is actually part of the preaching of the Kingdom. This preaching is not complete if the mandate to perform miracles is not carried out.

> They (the miracles) are to be understood as manifestations of the reign of God, actively present in Jesus, and as such eschatological signals of the coming action of God through the resurrection. Opposed to the successful establishment of the Kingdom are the forces of this world, the demonic-satanic power, sin, sickness, death.[14]

These forces of the other kingdom are to be overcome because Jesus has conquered them.

The ministry of proclamation is therefore incomplete if it cannot be certified through the act of healing. The miracles, as the apostles performed them, certainly were not limited to that time possibly on the basis of a stronger faith of the apostles or because at that time no other means were known against these forces except magic. It also is not true that we are far superior to that time and therefore such acts of healing are no longer necessary. We know that unrecorded deeply-felt sorrow exists and that man even today also needs a Savior, just as at that time.

Our medical science has not been able to make miracles superfluous nor to replace them. It has not only brought healing from sicknesses but has also introduced new maladies. Progress has not only enlightened man; it has also entangled him in worse demonic forces. The temptation that comes through sickness and death has remained. Thus obviously we cannot simply substitute the sciences as a gift of God for the supernatural conquest of human woes. They will never succeed in warding off sicknesses and death from mankind and in eliminating the demonic forces. In works of Christian

[14] Walter Künneth, *Theologie der Auferstehung* (Munich: Claudius, 1951), p. 110.

mercy and in the foreign mission we have sought a link with scientific progress believing that thereby we could replace our authorization for healing; and often do not suspect how we have submitted to demonic laws.

The mission, too, has thought that through medical missions, schools, education, and social work it could carry out the second part of the missionary command. The mission undertook these endeavors to prepare the way for real missionary service — to gain a hearing for the message, and did not consider that this second part of the missionary command already presupposes faith. From the Anglo-Saxon viewpoint people even thought that it was possible to make the kingdom of God a reality on earth. Men were offered false hopes. In some missions the proclamation was at best a supplement to social work. Thus, of necessity it came to pass that these arrangements in the mission contributed towards giving man everything without his thereby being pledged to God. The mission had itself cooperated in the spread of secularism. Moreover, the second part of the missionary command cannot be replaced by the erection of pilgrimage shrines. Even if faith in the saints expresses the continuity of the church (regardless of the context of the history of religion), not living witnesses but the dead are active here.

Is not this the basic evil, that though the church indeed believes in the Holy Ghost, He is not a reality to her anymore? Are we not hindering Him constantly by our theology, because we obviously think that only that can be of the Holy Ghost which is in harmony with our thinking, our stereotyped church ordinances and with science?

To be sure, today the church has realized that here is an evident deficiency, a halfway quality in her ministry. For that reason the discussion about the ministry of healing has arisen. Also, this second part of the missionary command must not be wrongly understood. The word "all" which we find in the first part of the missionary command is missing in the second. That is significant. Jesus Himself neither healed all the sick nor raised all the dead; nor did He give the command that this be done. He also did not drive out the devils from every possessed man. If we would strive for a general application, we would drag the command down into the human realm.

In Jesus' day life played a much less important role than it does in our eyes. To us bodily well-being has become even more important than God's commandments. Instead, Jesus took suffering, in its meaning for man, much more seriously. For Him it was a pathway to the salvation of man. He also knew that with the removal of suffering the other kingdom had not as yet been eliminated. It could at any time break in again if the presuppositions for the miracle had not been given. But what He aimed at and what His disciples should do was to erect signs of the Kingdom and thereby reveal to the world that the other kingdom had in reality been conquered. Thus the proclamation was verified that He is the Lord of lords and at the same time the Lord over human life. He uses miracles not to help man achieve an autonomous humanity but precisely to break the autonomy of a world separated from God and to bind men to God. The second part of the missionary command must be viewed within these limits.

13. The Church as Goal

Thus the clear line of faith has been drawn. Where there is no faith, a barrier arises against the successful execution of the missionary command. Not all men allow themselves to be led to faith and so be saved. As long as the Gospel will be preached, it will be true that through the Word of God men must be called out of their environment and out of their community. Thereby Christianity moves into opposition against all other religions.

Where association by religion and natural birth are co-

123

extensive, no special congregation is necessary for religion. That is also the case where the religious association is larger than the national community. But the preaching of the Gospel erects a barrier between men because all those who have come to faith are gathered into a special way of life — the congregation. The Christian congregation is something unique in the world of religions. Through it a sign of the kingdom of God on earth also comes into existence. The congregation is the association of those who in faith have entrusted themselves to their Lord and who live in anticipation of Him.

Her members also belong to the nation. She partakes of this life; she influences the nation through her proclamation and through her other life; she vicariously brings the nation to God. Nevertheless, she is an entity *sui generis* with her own principles for growth. She belongs to her Lord and yet He has placed her so that her allegiance to the nation is important also for her. If she would and could detach herself from Him, then she would at one and the same time be a po-litical-social unit and would no longer be distinguished from the heathen forms of religion. However, if she were to form a single community of faith with the nation, then she would no longer be a congregation of Jesus Christ. Her dual membership constitutes her special character.

Through God's Word and through the association of the disciples with one another she is subordinate solely to her Lord, and starting out from Him she must now go her way under the command of God either with the people or even against the people. But she cannot detach herself from the nation. She has a part in the national life and yet as a congregation she cannot accept for herself the nation's boundaries, for she belongs to the one church of Jesus Christ and has her brothers and sisters among all nations. Obviously, she must suffer in the course of the world's history, but she is not subject to this in the same way as are the nations, for she always

124

stands in a continuity which proceeds from Jesus Christ and leads to His coming.

In this church are gathered the children of God from all lands, joined in faith to the one Lord (John 11:52). There are people of different races in her midst, but these differences do not assert themselves. Even though she can assemble only in local congregations and thereby bears human characteristics, yet she lives according to the laws of the one church. The peculiarities of her human dress are not the decisive factors, but the common faith and the one Lord, who has riches for all (Rom. 10:12; Col. 3:11). She is in this life and she cooperates according to her own laws in its structuring, but she does not accommodate herself to that life as men would desire to fashion it according to their own ideals.

> And when the church has become a body in which the old national and social differences have been abolished, then she anticipates the new people of God who are under the government of the heavenly κύριος, and who await His παρουσία, His triumphal royal entry.[15]

14. The Significance of Baptism for the Mission

The appropriation of salvation always takes place in such a way that a believer is enrolled in the church and through her gains a group of fellow believers who with him serve the same Lord. This oneness of the church is given through the one faith as well as through the one Baptism, through which the church on earth visibly takes on form. Not faith alone, not the Word alone, not the worship of Christ alone reveal the special position of the church in the world, otherwise the millions of secret worshipers of Christ in India or Japan or among the Mohammedans would have to belong to the church — but Baptism is the one thing that accomplishes this. Those secret "Christians" immediately refuse Baptism be-

[15] R. Liechtenhan, *Die urchristliche Mission* (Göttingen: Vandenhoeck and Ruprecht, 1946), p. 46.

cause they do not want to give up their oneness with the nation and its religion. Baptism will separate them from both. It is the sign of the Kingdom among the nations and this makes it an act of confession to Christ before the world. Baptism shows all the world that the believers are willing to be joined to the Lord and thereby it separates them from the old religious community.

It is significant that Baptism is understood exactly in this way by the heathen while we Christians are always hesitant to recognize this external side of Baptism as important. The heathen generally do not object if their countrymen hear the Word of God or if they honor Christ. Their religion makes room for that. However, when anyone permits himself to be baptized, the heathen become intolerant. Then the resistance sets in. Thus Baptism becomes for the heathen the evidence that the persons baptized have driven a wedge into heathendom and the nation. Through Baptism the Lord makes His church a unique reality in the world.

> Baptism appears from the beginning as a decisive act for enrollment in the congregation and as a self-evident, undebatable matter. Therein also lies a permanence of the tradition which refers them to the will of the Risen One.[16]

Gustav Warneck, even if in an unclear way, emphasizes Baptism as the means of mission, because on the one hand (as Duerr points out) he wants to acknowledge the objective efficacy of Baptism and, on the other hand, because of course he stresses conversion more strongly. Hoekendijk, however, hardly mentions the sacraments and ascribes to them no constructive character. That is all the more surprising, since precisely through Baptism, which through teaching produces discipleship, the congregation becomes evident as an eschatological reality. Through Baptism the church of the last times

---

[16] Liechtenhan, p. 46.

will be brought into existence out of all nations. The apostle places heavy emphasis on this. (1 Cor. 12:13; Gal. 3:28)

The believers belong to the body of Christ through Baptism. Unbelievers and unbaptized do not have a share in this body. Through Baptism the congregation of Jesus Christ comes into existence among all nations and thus becomes the proof that mankind as the property of God, in its sin and in its redemption, is a unit. Through it the congregation becomes at the same time the token of the promise that God will produce this unit even though it be through judgment.

Thereby we have made basic statements concerning Baptism as such, for this external human side is only a result of that which Christ through Baptism gives to His believers. The objection is raised that this gift of Christ in Baptism can also be nothing else than what has been communicated through the Word. Everything that is ascribed to the Sacrament in Scripture is also given by the Word. Yet thereby the other kind of transmission is bypassed. The Word can be heard or ignored, taken seriously or avoided. But in the sacraments every single individual is personally placed before a decision and must permit God to deal with him. He can pretend; he can, for the sake of tradition, do this, but he cannot by such conformity escape the action of God. Through this action of God the sacraments always become the realized Word which has the distinguishing marks of grace and judgment.

Baptism is first of all the token of the new covenant and incorporates the baptized into the new nation of God. It is therefore not a superficial act of reception into the congregation, which is what many missions have made of it. It took the place of circumcision (Col. 2:11). It is precisely the converted heathen who emphasize the covenant character of Baptism. It is for them a sign of the faithfulness of God who has visibly received the believers into His fellowship. They know that in their total personal appropriation of the reconciliation through Christ they have become God's own (Eph. 1:14; Titus 2:14). Because all this is done in Baptism by God, no one can pluck the baptized out of His Hand. Nobody can annul Baptism or replace it. The baptized can decide only whether the act of God on his behalf should be an act of grace or of judgment.

However, it is through the blood of the covenant that the baptized person becomes the property of God. In Baptism everything that Christ through cross and resurrection has done for him is given to the believer. The baptized have put on Christ, i. e. they now have part in everything in Christ. The history of their new life is actually their history with Jesus (Rom. 6:3-5), and because they, in faith, permit this Christ event to be repeated in them, they may also rejoice, as fully redeemed, in the consummation. (Titus 3:5-7; 1 Peter 1:3 f.)

To maintain the believers' faith in the new life, Baptism creates the fellowship of the baptized, the church. Through Baptism they have become the body of Christ or a temple in which, through Christ's act of salvation, they are so intimately connected with Christ that they can also among themselves enjoy the fellowship of the new life. Here they are to be under love so that one member bears the other along and becomes for him a helper to life. As a congregation they are ever and again hearers of the Word; they assemble for prayer and praise. The new life is not rootless. It must constantly be nourished by the gifts which God offers to His church. Through its divine services the church places herself again and again on the side of God in a hostile world. In the church of the baptized the rule of God and the new life connected with it becomes visible. (Heb. 9:4; Eph. 4:13; Phil. 3:12; Gal. 3:27)

To become a believer is therefore only a first goal. The

next step is to live in the church as a believer and in her and with her to serve the Lord. Thereby it is implied that the kingdom of God can exist only *in actu*. The word of the covenant, the sign of the covenant, are constitutive factors. Thereby self-evidently it is not said that the Kingdom is identical with the church. Quite apart from the fact that there are also hypocrites among the baptized, the kingdom of God is much larger than the empiric church. To be sure, this church can always be only a provisional form or a transitional state. If she would think about this, she would orientate herself more to the coming kingdom, and not exhaust herself in "churchianity."

15. *The Lord's Supper and Mission*

In order to nourish the new life created in Baptism, to preserve the believers in the gifts of salvation, to strengthen their fellowship, and to bind them closer to the Lord, Christ has given the Lord's Supper as a covenant meal. We would, however, not understand this adequately if we saw in it only the means of edification. Also the Lord's Supper bears the mission character.

> Through the act of Holy Communion, Jesus wants to interpret the meaning of His death and reveal the universal meaning of the covenant based on Him. At the same time He wants to commit the partakers, when they receive and enjoy the bread and wine, to faithfulness and to the subsequent inclusion of many. To that extent one can designate the Last Supper as the moment of birth for the mission to the heathen.[17]

A fact that seems to us even more important than this daring accentuation of the Lord's Supper is the fact that the Lord's Supper sharply sets the church of the Lord's Supper apart from the world and from the nation together with its religion. The Lord's Supper is not only the expression of the

[17] Liechtenhan, p. 40.

innermost association between the exalted and returning Lord with the members of His body; it not only achieves an association of the members among each other based on the forgiveness so that in the highest degree it constitutes the congregation, but it also distinguishes the believers from the rest of the people. In all nations the communion meal is the expression of fellowship of those who have the same faith and on the basis of forgiveness live at peace with one another.

In the Lord's Supper it becomes plain that association with Christ excludes every other association. Therefore Paul according to 1 Cor. 10 and 11 could use the Lord's Supper for the sharpest combat against heathendom, the association with demons, in short, the other kingdom. At the same time through the Lord's Supper the church again and again becomes the confessing church. Through this celebration she makes known to the world the once-for-all redemption. (1 Cor. 11:26)

Thus the gifts of God in the sacraments also have a dual aspect: They serve the salvation of men and are at the same time the content of the testimony of the saved. Therefore the sacraments are of great significance for mission work among the nations.[18]

16. The Church as an Entity Sui Generis

All these missionary means, these gifts of God, set the church apart from its environment. It is a mystery that through these mission means the church actually makes the strongest impression on its environment when she herself desires to be nothing else than a church of the Lord which came into existence through these mission means. The more she wants to be this and only this, the more she will make her

[18] Walter Freytag, "Die Sakramente auf dem Missionsfeld," *Evangelische Missionszeitschrift,* 1940.

influence felt by the world. Through her witness the nations will gradually be Christianized.

Hence the question arises here: How does the church relate herself to the nation when once it has been Christianized? Even when all members of a nation have been baptized, the boundary between church and nation is not abolished even in the national church, for the dividing line does not run between Christian and non-Christians, but between faith and unbelief and hence within the church. Through sin which also works its way into the congregation there will always be tares among the wheat. Therefore the congregation will also be compelled ever and again to draw the line also in a Christianized nation, when such a link does not by itself appear in her life. She confronts her nation in such a way that she again and again woos the lukewarm and indifferent to draw them into her life.

However, the sharpest line of separation comes through church discipline which, to be sure, should never be regarded as a punishment, but as a means of love. Church discipline is not a legalistic action, but it is care of souls in concrete form. Through church discipline the church not only opposes herself to unbelief, but she thereby always gathers herself about the Lord. For that reason discipline is at the same time an expression of the testimony. It is not surprising that discipline and missions are intimately connected. Where through discipline the knowledge is kept alive that men must be saved, it is not difficult for the church to confront the world in the apostolate. At the same time, the mission in the congregation thereby also receives the will to show concern for the erring and indifferent.

[V]

THE CHURCH OF SALVATION

1. The Church and the Kingdom of God

THE LORD GATHERS His believers into His congregation and keeps them there in His service through Word and Sacrament. Thus the congregation becomes the bearer of the revelation in the world. She possesses something that others do not have. She knows the will of God. She knows about the power of prayer and has the gift of eternal life. This congregation now also receives through Baptism the authorization for testifying of God to her fellowmen. God also gives her the gifts for the task.

He forces no one into His new creation. God begins with something that He has placed in men by His creation and now makes use of this gift through the operation of His Spirit for the church and for the welfare of men. And there are within the congregation a multiplicity of gifts and talents. None of these gifts, however, should exalt the one and enslave the other. In the kingdom of God this law of the world is no longer valid. The more gifts one has from God, the more he is called to minister and to witness. All that we can do in the kingdom of God is to express our gratitude, returning in the form of service the gifts which He has given to us.

Through Baptism we have also become citizens of the Kingdom. But we must not make the mistake of equating the church with the Kingdom. We must be aware that this kingdom still is concealed among us. The church belongs to the Kingdom, but it does not present it in its greatness, fullness, and glory. The Kingdom is much greater than the congregation because the church of all times, of the angels, and of the whole world of God belongs to it; and yet also the congregation may be included. (Rev. 1:6)

One must not expect that the kingdom of God can be made visible through the congregation and that everything the church does and represents is an expression of the kingdom of God. Insofar as Satan may break into the church, she too still belongs to the other kingdom; and yet also the kingdom of God is present in her if she lives a life of faith in Christ's atoning death and resurrection. In the faith and in the witness the victory of Jesus Christ becomes evident, and yet it is also concealed in her because only the eyes of faith can see it.

Even though the Kingdom is still hidden in the congregation because of her weakness and because of the otherness of God's way of acting, yet she may still sense that it is a kingdom of power because it creates new life in the person who has come to faith (1 Cor. 4:20). It is present in the congregation, and thereby among men, to the extent that God works directly and men permit themselves to be called to Him. But it will first become fully present when Jesus Christ returns with power (Mark 9:1). The congregation lives always in a provisional stage of the Kingdom. Therefore her witness and ministry must be performed under the sign of the coming kingdom and in hope.

2. The Church of the Apostolate

Through the endowment with the Holy Ghost the church has been called to witness to the coming kingdom. Every baptized person has the duty and authority for such witness. The tension between the mission and the younger church could become an issue only because the mission did not take seriously the gifts of Baptism and therewith also denied baptized members equal rights to minister. The mission had not understood that Baptism equipped the converted heathen with the same gifts as other members of the kingdom of Christ and thus with the same rights and obligations.

It was therefore practically a disfranchisement and subordination of the younger churches that they were not trained for the spreading of the Kingdom and admitted to it by the mission. They were deprived of doing mission work, as if the kingdom of God were dependent on the proof of a certain level of culture! In this way the mission had to appear as a prerogative of the older Christianity and therewith as the churchly expansion of the western world. Many complaints against the mission would not have arisen if it had understood that in missionary service, and therewith in the apostolate, the life of the congregation in membership with the body of Christ finds its expression.

Where the congregation is not permeated by the apostolate, where authority to witness is denied to her and no freedom of ministry is granted to her, there she cannot return the gifts which God has bestowed on her. She must therefore languish in her life as she continually struggles to receive these gifts. In other words, the mystery of these gifts is that they only put in their appearance where they can fulfill their assignment.

The result is that the hearing and worshiping congregation continually asks for these gifts and has no inkling that God answers these prayers in overabundance where faith is allowed to become obedience. Because this is the case, we have actually a pleasure-seeking Christendom, which exhausts itself in edification and constructing, but never becomes the living building [Eph. 2]. So long as the ministry of the office is performed only under the aspect of taking care of the church, it can have no influence on the outside world. For that reason we experience so little of the power of the Kingdom. Much as hearing the Word and praising God in the liturgy belong to the proper worship of God and thus to the faith, yet these really achieve their fullness and purpose only when they permit themselves to be used in the sending. Where the possibility of service and obedience is hampered, there life is crippled.

The ministry of the congregation is the counterpart to its salvation and its position in the world. Both of these are determined eschatologically by the return of Christ and by the Judgment. Salvation is there because there is judgment and damnation. Therefore the congregation must constantly call attention to that whereby salvation is given. In Jesus Christ she is the decisive fact in the history of mankind. We can therefore fulfill the witness of the Kingdom only by proclaiming the promise of the Kingdom as we say that it has already come. Therefore the church with its knowledge of salvation is placed in the service of revelation and rescue. She has become the church of salvation through Jesus Christ and can therefore bring salvation also to the nations.

3. The Witness

Through Baptism Christians receive the same witnessing role that was already given in primitive Christianity. We can indeed not be witnesses of facts in the sense that we might be eyewitnesses. We can only witness to what has been given to us in faith. But faith is the substance of things hoped for. Therefore Christians are genuine witnesses of the truth; what Jesus Christ has accomplished according to the Scripture has for them become incontrovertible certainty and their personal conviction. Thus Christians can transmit the conviction made alive in them by faith as the truth that happened in Jesus Christ and witness it before the world. When the congregation proclaims the truth, she must, however, be conscious of the fact that by confronting the world with the truth she herself is placed before the question of her own existence.

Precisely in the witnessing of the truth it becomes clear that in the last analysis it is God who carries His mission forward and uses the congregation in the ministry of salvation. For it is He who through His revelation enters into judgment with men. Every serious proclamation leads the messenger into a situation of judgment. Herein he must appear as God's witness. This leads to a judgment upon men. God contends with men (Is. 43:9-13; 44:7-11). He summons the nations into court where it will be decided whether He is God. In this court the members of God's congregation should be His witnesses (Is. 43:10; 44:8). The witness of the congregation indicts the guilty hearer of the message.

This situation became most evident in the Passion of Jesus and in the court proceedings which the apostles had to endure (Acts 4:5; 7:12). At first the messengers always appear as the accused; but they always make themselves accusers because they cannot assert anything without appealing to the Lord and His revelation, so that the ones who are doing the judging become those who are judged. Accordingly, in the last analysis it is God who leads men into judgment through His congregation and who pronounces the verdict. However, already in the judgment which it renders, the message of the Gospel becomes the message of rescue.

4. The Church of Suffering

God's contention with men is, like His other acts, a sign of His royal rule over men. As King and Lord He could destroy men, but for the time being He only summons them to an accounting. Also here He takes the road of foolishness and weakness, which in this case again proves itself wiser and more salutary than all the prudence of men. God leads the men whom He desires to gain into judgment in this way that He leads His church into suffering. But in the suffering of the church the depravity of men, their lies, their selfishness, their brutality, the power of sin and the prevailing demonic power ever and again become apparent. The Lord of the church reveals Himself in such a way that He Himself suffers with His own and then this suffering permits men in their wickedness and antigodliness to come to naught. For that reason through the suffering of Christians their message and their suffering become a μαρτύριον, a witness of the truth.

Thus Christ's redemptive death becomes a witness for God (1 Tim. 2:6). Viewed in such a way, suffering is not a defeat, but the most aggressive accusation which God levels against the world; it is the most powerful attack on the world. The tribulations of the church are a proof that God in His mission is at work in a special way to gain men. In times of suffering God desires to use the church in a special way as an instrument of the apostolate. He wants to advance His salvation history a step further among mankind.

Therefore these times of suffering are also periods in which the promises to His church find fulfillment in a special way. These periods enable the church to let herself be used as she enters into suffering. It is part of the sobriety of revelation that God has not left His church under any illusions; He has not promised that redemption should run its course in a eudaemonistic sense or that Christians might expect a good life on the basis of their conversion. On the contrary, He did not leave the church in the dark that His church must suffer for His sake and just by telling her this He reveals Himself as the true God. (Matt. 10:17 ff.; Mark 13:9-13; John 16:1 ff.)

Thus God also enters into opposition to other religions which promise their followers well-being and regard suffering as a proof that man does not enjoy the favor of the gods. In all heathen religions life is an outcome of religion, and in

137

nearly all of them happiness is equated with salvation. God, however, does not redeem from suffering, but through Jesus Christ He redeems in the midst of suffering and thereby gives to suffering a special meaning in His plan of salvation, also for individuals. Thereby He makes suffering a special privilege for His church, a suffering with Christ (1 Peter 4:12 ff.; Acts 4:41). We know that the suffering of many may also have another meaning. It may have been brought about by sin. It could be caused by the fact that Christians are involved in the fate of their nation. We need not pursue that here. Suffice it to say that the suffering of the church always has a special meaning because she is God's property and instrument.

Actually she can travel no other road than the one which the Lord Himself traveled (Rom. 8:17). Through this suffering the church takes part in the rule of Christ and thereby becomes an eschatological reality in which the signs of the last time become especially evident. She does not escape these signs, but therein she receives her mandate to suffer vicariously for the world. She is reconciled to God and therefore always engaged in the ministry of reconciliation. It is precisely in suffering that she repeatedly testifies to her special position in the world and thereby proves that she is willing to submit herself with her whole existence to the Lord.

The suffering of the church has greater witnessing power than the Word alone. It becomes the witness in deed, a confirmation of the Word. For that reason the martyrs always occupy first place among the witnesses. The flight from suffering was therefore always rightfully regarded as apostasy, as denial of the Lord. Refusing to suffer is equated with rejecting the mission of the church. She thereby separates herself from the body of Christ (Luke 24:14 ff.). Therefore the primary assignment of the ministry is to prepare the church for the times of suffering (Acts 14:22), even as the Lord referred His disciples to this ultimate witness.

In this suffering the church may have the assurance that the Lord who preceded her on the way of suffering will give her His presence in a special way. In this way He joins her in the sending of the church for a special effectiveness within the framework of the *missio Dei* (John 15:28 f.; Matt. 10:20, 21; John 14:26; Luke 12:11 f.). He does this by being near her with His Spirit and thereby places Himself again and again into judgment, and goes into suffering along with the church.

It is peculiar that the newer theology of missions speaks about the suffering of the congregation and endeavors to clear up the situation of the church, yet hardly enters upon a discussion of the salvation history and eschatological meaning of suffering. Today we have a Christianity that shies away from suffering, which still goes on dreaming of a Christianized world, appeals to the rights of man and the freedom of conscience and wants to put them into operation; all this in order to escape suffering and to make that suffering impossible instead of recognizing her call to suffer. Suffering does not fit into the church's need for security nor into the modern philosophy of men. It also does not agree with the ideas which most people have of the kingdom of God.

The thought of suffering appears in contemporary theology only where there is occasion to speak of the little flock, of the remnant which the church will represent at the end of time. Even then one speaks only about the apostolate but not about suffering. Therefore the question arises whether the reference to the remnant, which really looks reality in the eye, is not a desperate retreat to the last possibility for the survival of the church.

The Lord has not left us in the dark about the fact that

139

the world will always question the church's right to exist. The Book of Revelation in terrifying fashion shows the pathway of the church through the world. She will always be a persecuted, attacked, and suffering congregation. She will always find herself in the status of an alien and a wanderer (1 Peter 2:11). For her the pilgrim people of God are always the prototype. Precisely through this wandering, God arrives with His church at the goal of the *missio Dei;* and precisely therein it becomes evident that God daily bestows His presence on His congregation till the end of the world. There are, above all, three essential characteristics of the message which makes the congregation appear homeless and dangerous to worldly government.

1. Through the special position given her in Baptism the congregation is proof that there is still another lord — the Lord of heaven and earth, whom all men must serve and according to whose will the church is to be ruled. Thereby the congregation becomes a witness against a government which acts in an absolute way. Through her presence and through the ordering of her life, the congregation always points to the one Lord to whom also the government is responsible. Thereby she destroys the dream that the welfare of society could be the ultimate and decisive factor and that this could be brought about only in the way in which the rulers, on the basis of their position, would want to have it.

2. The congregation is the body of Christ and thereby has fellowship with all members of His body. Whoever does not identify himself with the congregation of the Lord in the entire world and works against it also cannot belong to the body of Christ. The congregation cannot pay attention to any national, ethnic, and racial opinion. On the contrary, she must destroy them if she does not want to become unfaithful to the brotherhood founded through the death of Jesus.

3. There is an eternal responsibility and, through the rule

of Jesus and His return, a judgment. Man can regard himself as a sovereign master only so long as the Second Coming is not yet an accomplished fact. When he tries to hinder the proclamation of judgment and damnation he can thereby only reject Christ and His salvation. Before the judgment message all self-redemption, all nihilism, and all brutalization collapses. The preaching of judgment opens the eyes to the way things really hang together.

For these reasons no other alternative is left for the world but to take a stand against the congregation and by rejection, limitation, and attacks to lead her into suffering. The world believes that by these means it is able to thwart the message of the congregation, the proclamation of the truth, which is foolishness to her. God is so great that He makes even this attitude of the world serve His *missio*. Because His rule is different from that of the world, the witness of the congregation must shine forth all the more clearly through suffering.

In the last analysis this is the point where the decisive battle between the rule of God and the rule of the devil, which reaches its apex in the Antichrist, is waged. In this contest which in the midst of all the joy over the success of missions gives us the necessary sobriety, the mission becomes the opponent of the Antichrist (2 Thess. 2:6). Therefore the suffering of the church must again and again become visible in a special way in the mission.

The congregation can endure this suffering and thereby carry out her witness with courage only because she can have the certainty that God is leading her to her final goal through His mission. Through this hope the congregation is inwardly separated from the world in which she must live in order to carry out her testimony. She knows that in this struggle the world will not have the last word, but the Lord will, who suffers with His congregation and terminates the battle through His intervention. Therefore the congregation does not do battle for the world, but for the Kingdom to which she already belongs through the death and resurrection of Jesus. She is already translated to the heavenly kingdom (Eph. 2:5). Therefore she sets her affections on the things which are above (Col. 3:1) and seeks the heavenly Jerusalem as her home (Heb. 12:22). She is thereby placed into the church of all ages which has already traveled this way with her. This overwhelming hope is the supporting foundation for the attitude of the congregation.

The suffering of the congregation culminates in the redemption which is bestowed when Jesus Christ ushers in His Kingdom. With this God concludes His *missio*. Then the congregation has fulfilled her assignment. Then she may sing the song of victory of the redeemed, not as a ruling congregation, not as a congregation which can report great missionary results, not as a triumphant congregation, but as a congregation that has been overcome, which participates through redemption in the victory of Jesus (Rom. 8:31 ff.). Then she may also share the glory of her Lord, who in His *missio* traveled the way of the cross. Then the perfect fellowship with God will be restored again. Then God has come to the goal with His *missio*. In the new creation mission will no longer be necessary. But the mission is now, in the interim between the Ascension and the Parousia, all the more urgent because the mission alone can proclaim the way into fellowship with God to the many people who stand outside the congregation of Jesus. The mission alone can rescue them from judgment.

BIBLIOGRAPHY

Allen, Roland. *The Ministry of the Spirit: Selected Writings.* Ed. by David M. Paton. London: World Dominion Press, 1960.
———. *Missionary Methods: St. Paul's or Ours?* 5th ed. London: World Dominion Press, 1960.
———. *Missionary Principles.* Grand Rapids: Wm. B. Eerdmans Publishing Co., 1964.
Andersen, Wilhelm. *Auf dem Weg zu einer Theologie der Mission.* Gütersloh: Bertelsmann, 1957.
———. "Die kerygmatische Begruendung der Religions- and Missionswissenschaft," *Evangelische Missionszeitschrift* (1954).
———. *Towards a Theology of Mission.* London: SCM Press, 1955.
Anderson, Gerald H., ed. *The Theology of the Christian Mission.* New York: McGraw-Hill, 1961.
Barth, Karl. *Kirchliche Dogmatik.* 10 vols. Munich: Chr. Kaiser Verlag, 1932–.
Beaver, R. Pierce. *From Missions to Mission.* New York: Association Press, 1964.
———. *Envoys of Peace.* Grand Rapids: Wm. B. Eerdmans Publishing Co., 1964.
———. *Ecumenical Beginnings in Protestant World Mission.* New York: Nelson, 1962.
Beyerhaus, Peter, and Henry Lefever. *The Responsible Church and the Foreign Mission.* Grand Rapids: Wm. B. Eerdmans Publishing Co., 1964.
Blauw, Johannes. *Goden en Mensen.* Groningen: J. Niemeijer, 1950.
———. "Mission lebt von der Kirche," *Die Botschaft von Jesus Christus in einer nichtchristlichen Welt.* N. p., 1952.
———. *The Missionary Nature of the Church: A Survey of the Biblical Theology of Mission.* London: Lutterworth Press, 1962.
Bonhoeffer, Dietrich. *Die Nachfolge.* Munich: Chr. Kaiser Verlag,

1952. (English: *The Cost of Discipleship.* New York: The Macmillan Company, 1959.)

Cullmann, Oscar. *Christ and Time.* Trans. Floyd V. Filson. Philadelphia: Westminster Press, c. 1950.

———. *Christus und die Zeit.* Zurich: Zollikon, 1946.

———. *Peter: Disciple — Apostle — Martyr; A Historical and Theological Study.* Trans. Floyd V. Filson. Philadelphia: Westminster Press, 1953.

———. *Petrus: Jünger — Apostel — Märtyrer; das historische und das theologische Petrusproblem.* Zurich: Zwingli Verlag, 1952.

Danker, William J. *Two Worlds or None: Rediscovering Missions.* St. Louis: Concordia Publishing House, 1964.

Decker, J. W., Norman Goodall, and C. W. Ranson. *The Witness of a Revolutionary Church.* New York: International Missionary Council, 1947.

DeQuervain, A. "Der Ewige König," *Theologische Existenz Heute* 1958.

Dürr, Johannes. *Sendende und werdende Kirche in der Missionstheologie G. Warnecks.* Basel: Basler Missionsbuchhandlung, 1947.

Elert, Werner. *Der christliche Glaube.* Berlin: Furche-Verlag, 1955.

Foerster, W. *Herr ist Jesus.* Gütersloh: C. Bertelsmann Verlag, 1924.

Forman, Charles W. *The Nation and the Kingdom: Christian Mission in the New Nations.* New York: Friendship Press, 1964.

Freytag, Walter. *The Gospel and the Religions.* London: SCM Press, 1957.

———, ed., *Mission zwischen Gestern und Morgen.* Stuttgart: Evangelischer Missionsverlag, 1952.

———. "Vom Sinn der Weltmission," *Evangelische Missionszeitschrift* (1950).

Fridrichsen, Anton. *The Apostle and His Message.* Uppsala: Lundequistaka, 1947.

Gensichen, Hans Werner. *Missionsgeschichte der neueren Zeit.* Göttingen: Vandenhoeck und Ruprecht, 1961.

Goodall, Norman. *Missions Under the Cross.* London: Edinburgh House Press, 1953.

Heim, Karl. *Leben aus Glauben.* Berlin: Furche-Verlag, 1934.

——. "Die Struktur des Heidentums," *Evangelische Missions-Magazin* (1939).

Hempel, J. "Die Wurzeln des Missionswillens im Glauben des Alten Testaments," *Zeitschrift für die alttestamentliche Wissenschaft,* LXVI.

Hoekendijk, J. C. *Kerk en Volk in de duitse Zendingswetenschap.* Utrecht: Proefschrift, 1948.

——. "Die Kirche im Missionsdenken," *Evangelische Missionszeitung* (1952).

Holsten, Walter. *Das Kerygma und der Mensch.* Munich: Chr. Kaiser Verlag, 1953.

International Missionary Council, Madras Series, I. *The Authority of the Faith.* New York: International Missionary Council, 1939.

Jeremias, J. *Jesu Verheissung für die Völker.* Stuttgart: W. Kohlhammer Verlag, 1956.

——. *Jesus' Promise to the Nations.* Trans. S. H. Hooke. Naperville, Ill.: Alec R. Allenson, 1958.

Knak, Siegfried. "Neutestamentliche Missionstexte nach neuerer Exegese," *Theologia Viatorum* (1953/1954).

——. "Oekumenischer Dienst in der Missionswissenschaft," *Theologia Viatorum* (1950).

Kraemer, Hendrik. *Religion and the Christian Faith.* London: Harper & Bros., 1956.

Künneth, Walter. *Politik zwischen Dämon und Gott.* Berlin: Lutherisches Verlagshaus, 1954.

——. *Theologie der Auferstehung.* Munich: Claudius, 1951.

Latourette, K. S., and Richard Hogg. *Tomorrow Is Here.* New York: Friendship Press, 1947.

Liechtenhan, R. *Die urchristliche Mission.* Göttingen: Vandenhoeck und Ruprecht, 1946.

Lohmeyer, Ernst. "Mir ist gegeben alle Gewalt," *In Memoriam Ernst Lohmeyer.* Ed. W. Schmauch. Stuttgart: Evangelisches Verlagswerk, 1951.

Lueking, F. Dean. *Mission in the Making.* St. Louis: Concordia Publishing House, 1964.

Lütgert, W. "Das Reich Gottes und die Mission," *NAMZ*, 1927.

———. "Reich Gottes und Weltgeschichte," *NAMZ*, 1928.

Luther, Martin. *D. Martin Luthers Werks.* Vol. XXI, 1928. Weimar: Herman Boehlaus Nachfolger.

MacGavran, Donald A. *The Bridges of God.* New York: Friendship Press, 1955.

Manikam, Rajah B. *Christianity and the Asian Revolution.* New York: Friendship Press, 1954.

Melzer, Friso. *Ihr sollt meine Zeugen sein,* 1955.

Michel, O. "Menschensohn und Völkerwelt," *Evangelische Missionszeitschrift* (1941).

Neill, Stephen Charles, BP. *The Unfinished Task.* London: Edinburgh House Press, 1958.

———. *Creative Tension.* London: Edinburgh House Press, 1959.

Northcott, Cecil. *Christian World Mission.* London: Lutterworth Press, 1952.

Oepke, Albrecht. *Das neue Gottesvolk.* Gütersloh: C. Bertelsmann, 1950.

Rengstorff, Karl Heinrich. ἀπόστολος, *"Theologisches Wörterbuch zum Neuen Testament.* I. Ed. Gerhard Kittel. Stuttgart: W. Kohlhammer Verlag, 1933.

———. μαθητής, *Theologisches Wörterbuch zum Neuen Testament.* IV. Ed. Gerhard Kittel. Stuttgart: W. Kohlhammer Verlag, 1942.

Scherer, James. *Missionary, Go Home!* Englewood Cliffs, N. J.: Prentice-Hall, 1964.

Schlier, H. "Die Entscheidung für die Heidenmission in der Urchristenheit," *Evangelische Missionszeitschrift* (1942).

Schmaus, M. *Katholische Dogmatik.* I. Westheim: Gangolf Ross Verlag, 1948.

Schmidt, Karl Ludwig. βασιλεία, *Theologisches Wörterbuch zum Neuen Testament.* I. Ed. Gerhard Kittel. Stuttgart: W. Kohlhammer Verlag, 1933.

———. ἔθνος, *Theologisches Wörterbuch zum Neuen Testament.* II. Ed. Gerhard Kittel. Stuttgart: W. Kohlhammer Verlag, 1933.

Schoonhoven, E. Jansen. "Wort und Tat im Zeugendienst," *Mission — Heute* (1954).

Stählin, G. "Die Endschau Jesu und die Mission," *Evangelische Missionszeitschrift* (1950).

Stauffer, Ethelbert. *New Testament Theology*. Trans. John Marsh. New York: Macmillan, 1956.

———. *Die Theologie des Neuen Testaments*. Hamburg: Friedrich Wittig, 1948.

Trimingham, J. Spencer. *The Christian Church and Islam in West Africa*. London: SCM Press, 1955.

———. "Die Christliche Kirche und der Islam," *Evangelische Missionszeitschrift*. Translated from English to German (1955).

———. *Islam in West Africa*. Oxford: Clarendon Press, 1959.

Vajta, Vilmos, and Hans Weissgerber, eds. *The Church and the Confessions*. Philadelphia: Fortress, 1963.

van Ruler, A. A. "Theologie des Apostolats," *Evangelische Missionszeitschrift* (1954).

Vicedom, Georg F. "Der innere Wandel der Religionen als Frage an unsere Verkündigung," *Theologische Literaturzeitung*, LXXXVII (January 1962), 14–19.

———. *Die Rechtfertiguung als gestaltende Kraft der Mission*. Neuendettelsau: Freimund Verlag, 1952.

Warneck, Gustav. *Evangelische Missionslehre*. III, 1. Gotha: F. A. Perthes, 1897.

Weber, O. *Bibelkunde des Alten Testaments*. Tübingen: Furche-Verlag, 1947.

Wendland, H. D. *Der Herr der Zeiten*. Gütersloh: C. Bertelsmann, 1936.

———. *Die Kirche in der modernen Gesellschaft*. Hamburg: Furche-Verlag, 1956.

INDEX

INDEX TO SCRIPTURE PASSAGES

155